From The Meadows of Gold

The ancient city of Baghdad, AD 915

MAS'ŪDĪ

From The Meadows of Gold

Translated by PAUL LUNDE
and CAROLINE STONE

GREAT
JOURNEYS

TED SMART

For Jaya and Sydney Bolt

PENGUIN BOOKS

Published by the Penguin Group
Penguin Books Ltd, 80 Strand, London WC2R ORL, England
Penguin Group (USA) Inc., 375 Hudson Street, New York, New York 10014, USA
Penguin Group (Canada), 90 Eglinton Avenue East, Suite 700, Toronto, Ontario, Canada M4P 2Y3
(a division of Pearson Penguin Canada Inc.)
Penguin Ireland, 25 St Stephen's Green, Dublin 2, Ireland (a division of Penguin Books Ltd)
Penguin Group (Australia), 250 Camberwell Road, Camberwell, Victoria 3124, Australia
(a division of Pearson Australia Group Pty Ltd)
Penguin Books India Pvt Ltd, 11 Community Centre, Panchsheel Park, New Delhi – 110 017, India
Penguin Group (NZ), 67 Apollo Drive, Rosedale, North Shore 0632, New Zealand
(a division of Pearson New Zealand Ltd)
Penguin Books (South Africa) (Pty) Ltd, 24 Sturdee Avenue, Rosebank, Johannesburg 2196, South Africa

Penguin Books Ltd, Registered Offices: 80 Strand, London WC2R ORL, England

www.penguin.com

First published 2007

3

Translation copyright © Paul Lunde and Caroline Stone, 2007
All rights reserved

The moral right of the translator has been asserted

Taken from the forthcoming Penguin Classics edition of *The Meadows of Gold*,
translated by Paul Lunde and Caroline Stone

Typeset by Rowland Phototypesetting Ltd, Bury St Edmunds, Suffolk
Printed in England by Clays Ltd, St Ives plc

ISBN: 978-0-141-02535-3

This edition produced for The Book People Ltd,
Hall Wood Avenue, Haydock, St. Helens, WA11 9UL

Mas'ūdī was born in Baghdād around the year AD 890 and died in Egypt in 956. Throughout his life he travelled incessantly, visiting the major cities of what are now Syria, Iraq, Palestine, Egypt, the Arabian Peninsula, Iran, Afghanistan, Pakistan and the west coast of India. Fascinated by religious diversity, he interviewed Jewish, Christian, Mazdaean, Zoroastrian and Hindu scholars, dispassionately recording their beliefs and discussing their sacred books. (The Arabic names for the peoples and places he describes are often used in this book, and their modern equivalents are given where known.) He was no less interested in the natural world, and collected intriguing information about the unusual natural phenomena, plants and animals that he encountered. He wrote thirty-six books, only two of which survive: *The Meadows of Gold and Mines of Precious Gems* [*Murūj al-Dhahab wa Ma'ādin al-Jawhar*] and the *Book of Admonition and Revision* [*Kitāb al-Tanbīh wa 'l-Ishrāf*], both notable attempts at 'global' history. All that we know of Mas'ūdī's life and travels is derived from what he himself tells us in these two books.

The selections that follow are overwhelmingly from *The Meadows of Gold*; a few are from the *Book of Admonition*. They have been chosen not only for their intrinsic interest, but to show the range of their author's interests and the extent of his travels. Mas'ūdī left his native Baghdād in 941 and took up residence in Fustāt in Egypt, the town that shortly after his death was transformed into the splendid Fatimid capital of Cairo. There he completed *The Meadows of Gold* in 943, and revised and augmented it in 947 and again shortly before his death in 956. All the surviving manuscripts of the work, however, represent the 947 revision. He finished his *Book of Admonition* in 956, a month before his death. It is an abridgement of *The Meadows of Gold*, but contains much new information, particularly about the Byzantine Empire. As the reader of these selections will see, Mas'ūdī frequently refers to the date he wrote or revised the passage in question, an inestimable help in tracing his intellectual and physical odyssey. (Many dates are given in both the Muslim and the Christian calendar, for example 336/947.) He also refers to descriptions not included in this selection, some in lost works. *The Meadows of Gold* is a long work, the standard edition filling five substantial volumes. This selection can only hint at the riches to be found in the life's work of the man who has been aptly described as 'the Arab Herodotus'.

Mas'ūdī was a late product of the 'Abbasid Renaissance', as brilliant and short-lived as its Italian counterpart. Both were inspired by contact with Greek philosophy and science and its tradition of free inquiry. This tradition inspired the humanist curiosity that made Mas'ūdī want to know more of what lay beyond the borders of the Islamic world and recover the memory of the ancient civilizations that had once flourished in the domain of Islam.

1. Mas'ūdī describes his aims and methods

We beg our readers' indulgence for any mistakes or
negligence which they may find in this book; for our
memory is weakened and our strength spent as a result
of the great weariness brought about by voyages which
have taken us by sea from one country to another and
by land across extensive desert. We have travelled the
world, by land and sea, avid to witness for ourselves all
that is remarkable among peoples and to see with our
own eyes the peculiarities of each country. With this
aim we have visited Sind [Pakistan], the land of the
Zanj [East Africa], Sanf [the kingdom of Champa,
now southern Vietnam], China and Zābaj [Sumatra].
Moving from east to west, we have journeyed from the
farthest limits of Khurāsān to the heart of Armenia, to
Azerbaijān, Arrān, and Baylaqān; one day we were in
Syria, another in Iraq. We can compare our course across
the world to the progress of the sun across the heavens,
and apply the following verses of the poet to ourselves:

> He has travelled the world in all directions;
> now in the farthest east, now in the west.
> Like the sun in its course, his journeys reach countries
>   so remote
> no caravan has ever dared penetrate them.

During our travels we have consorted with several kings, as different in their manners and their opinions as are the different geographical situations of their countries, and yet little by little we have found among them the same accord in recognizing that all traces of science have vanished and that its splendour is spent; learning has become too general and has lost its depth, and one no longer sees any but people filled with vanity and ignorance, imperfect scholars who are content with superficial ideas and do not recognize the truth.

We have been led to write our books on chronology and universal history and what occurred in the remote past in the time of the prophets, the lives of kings and their deeds, the different nations and their positions on the globe, by the desire to follow the path of wise and learned men, and have tried to leave to posterity a solid memorial built with art and skill. We have found some authors who came before us excellent, others inferior; some too prolix, others too concise. We have also found that the materials available have inexorably increased with the passage of time. Even the cleverest and most judicious minds have neglected extensive areas, each one specializing in a particular field. Every clime has peculiarities familiar to its inhabitants, but he who has never left his hearth and has confined his researches to the narrow field of the history of his own country cannot be compared to the courageous traveller who has worn out his life in journeys of exploration to distant parts and each day has faced danger in order to persevere in excavating the mines of learning and in snatching precious fragments of the past from oblivion.

2. *Mas'ūdī praises his birthplace*

I was born in the central clime of the world, and although the passing of days has separated us and my travels have taken me far away, I feel a great nostalgia for it in my heart, for it is my native land and my home.

It is in the clime of Bābil [Lower Iraq, ancient Babylonia]. This region was greatly esteemed by the kings of Persia and was the object of their solicitude. They passed their winters in Iraq and most of them spent the summer in the Jibāl [the mountainous region north-east of Baghdād], moving alternately from hot country to cold, depending on the season. Similarly, fashionable Muslims, such as Abū Dulaf al-Qāsim ibn 'Īsā al-'Ijlī, passed the winter in the warm area – that is to say, Iraq – and summer in the cool region – that is to say, the Jibāl. This is why Abū Dulaf said:

> I do as Chosroe did:
> summer in the Jibāl
> and winter in Iraq.

Indeed, this region unites every advantage: the earth is fertile, life is easy and everything is available in abundance. Its two benefactors, the Tigris and the Euphrates, bring it wealth; all its people are secure, knowing no ills. Lastly, it is the mansion of the sun, situated in the centre of the earth in the midst of the seven climes. Thus, the ancients compared its position in the world to that of the heart in the human body, for the world extends all around the clime of Bābil, whose inhabitants spread light in every direction on the meaning of things, just as knowledge emanates from the heart.

Thanks to this, its inhabitants have a smooth complexion and well-proportioned bodies. Among them one does not find the fair tones of the Byzantines and the Slavs, nor the black skin of the Abyssinians, nor the stockiness of the Berbers. Freed from the coarseness of other peoples, on the contrary, they unite what is best in every country; and just as they are distinguished by their outward beauty, so are they pre-eminent for their refinement and love of beautiful things.

The noblest position in this clime belongs to the city of Baghdād. How cruel Fortune was when she drove me from this noble city where I was born and from whose womb I sprang! But destiny loves to force these separations upon us and it is fate which imposes such exiles.

3. *The lighthouse of Hercules*

At the place where the Mediterranean joins the Atlantic Ocean there is a lighthouse of stone and copper built by the giant king Hercules. It is covered with inscriptions and statues whose hand gestures proclaim to those coming from the Mediterranean who wish to enter the Atlantic Ocean: 'There is no way beyond me.' Indeed, there is no way forward for those who enter it from the Mediterranean. Nothing moves upon it; there are no inhabited lands there or rational beings. Neither its extent nor where it ends are known; no one knows how far it reaches. It is called the Sea of Darkness, the Green Sea or the Encircling Sea. It is said that this lighthouse is not on this strait, but on one of the islands in the Encircling Sea, close to the coast.

Some people have gone so far as to claim that this sea is the source of all other seas. Wondrous tales are told of it, which we have set down in our *Historical Annals*: tales of men rash enough to risk their lives by setting sail on it, of those who died and those who survived, and what they saw and reported.

One of these was a man from al-Andalus called Khashkhāsh, one of the young bloods of Cordoba. He gathered together a group of young men from that city and sailed with them in a number of ships fitted out for sailing the Encircling Sea. After quite a long absence, they returned laden with booty. Their story is well known to the inhabitants of al-Andalus.

4. Driftwood proves all oceans are one

In the eastern Mediterranean, near the island of Crete, teak planks from ships have been found, pierced with holes and held together with fastenings made of coconut fibre. They come from wrecked vessels and have been driven there by the waves. This technique of boat construction is only found in the Sea of Abyssinia [the western Indian Ocean], for the vessels that sail the Mediterranean and those of the west all have nails, while in the Sea of Abyssinia iron nails do not hold because the water eats them away, making them corrode, until they become extremely weak. Hence, in order to join the planks, the boat builders use, instead of nails, coconut fibres soaked in tallow and lime.

This indicates – but God knows best – that all the seas intercommunicate and that the sea that lies off the coasts of China and al-Sīla [Korea] turns past the regions occupied by the Turks, and flows towards the seas of the west through some channel of the surrounding Ocean.

5. *The Galicians*

Among the nations that border al-Andalus, the strongest is that of the Galicians. Although the Franks are also at war with al-Andalus, the Galicians are a much fiercer foe.

'Abd al-Rahmān ibn Muhammad ['Abd al-Rahmān III, 912–61], the present ruler of al-Andalus, had a vizier who was his half-brother, named Ahmad ibn Ishāq. This vizier was guilty of a deed, which according to religious law demanded punishment. 'Abd al-Rahmān therefore had him arrested and put to death.

That vizier had a brother called Umayya, who lived in one of the Andalusian frontier towns, called Santarem. When he was told what had happened to his brother, he rebelled against 'Abd al-Rahmān and went over to Ramiro [Ramiro II, King of Leon, 932–50], the king of the Galicians, offering him his support against the Muslims and pointing out their weaknesses.

One day, when Umayya had ridden out of the town to hunt in one of his pleasure gardens, some of his freedmen seized the city, prevented him from entering it and wrote to inform 'Abd al-Rahmān what was going on. So Umayya ibn Ishāq, the brother of the vizier who had been put to death, went to Ramiro, who received him with all honour, appointed him minister and made him a member of his entourage.

Meanwhile, 'Abd al-Rahmān, the ruler of al-Andalus, attacked Zamora, the Galician capital. 'Abd al-Rahmān was at the head of more than 100,000 men. The battle which he fought with Ramiro, the king of the Galicians, took place in the month of Shawwāl in the year 327/July 939, three days after the solar eclipse that was visible in that month.

The Muslims prevailed at first; but the Galicians, finding themselves besieged and brought to bay within the town, returned to the charge and slaughtered 50,000 Muslims who had already crossed the moat.

It is said that it was Umayya ibn Ishāq who prevented Ramiro from pursuing those that fled, for he put it to the king that there was the danger of an ambush and inspired in him the desire to seize the valuables, equipment and treasure to be found in the Muslim camp. But for this, not a single Muslim would have survived. Umayya later asked pardon of 'Abd al-Rahmān and broke with Ramiro. 'Abd al-Rahmān received him most graciously.

After this battle, 'Abd al-Rahmān, the ruler of al-Andalus, sent troops against the Galicians under a number of commanders. There were wars in which the Galicians lost half as many men as had the Muslims in the first battle, and it is with the Muslims that the military advantage has rested until the present day.

As for Ramiro, he is still ruling the Galicians in this same year, 336/947. His predecessor on the throne was Ordoño [Ordoño II, 914–24] and before Ordoño was Alfonso [Alfonso III el Magno, 866–910]. The Franks and the Galicians belong to the Christian religion and follow the Melkite rite.

6. *The Franks*

The Franks, the Slavs, the Lombards, the Spaniards, Jūj Majūj [Gog Magog, the 'Enclosed Nations', who will be released upon the world on the Last Day], the Turks, the Khazars, the Burjān [the Bulghārs], the Alans, the Galicians and all the other nations which we have mentioned as inhabiting the northern regions are descended from Japhet, the youngest son of Noah, according to the uncontested opinion of thoughtful and learned men who study revealed scripture. Of all these people, the Franks are the most warlike, unassailable and numerous. They have the most extensive kingdom and many cities, and are the best organized and the most obedient to their rulers. The Galicians, however, are even more bellicose and to be feared, since a single Galician is the equal of a number of Franks.

The Franks are united under the authority of one king, and this system of rule is accepted by all, with no opposition or dissent. The capital of their empire at the present time is a large city named Barīza [Paris]. Furthermore, they possess some 150 towns, not counting the villages and provinces. Before the coming of Islam, the first land to be occupied by the Franks in the Mediterranean was the island of Rhodes, which I have already mentioned as near Alexandria and having in our times a shipyard belonging to the Byzantines; then the Island of Crete, which the Muslims took from the Franks and still control at present.

The Franks also possess the lands of Ifriqīya [Tunisia] and the island of Sicily. We have already mentioned these islands and in particular that which is known as *al-Burkān*. It is a volcano which throws up pieces of burning matter, looking rather like men's bodies, but headless. They are hurled into the air at night and then fall back into the sea and float on the surface of the water. These are the stones used to erase the writing from notebooks and burnish the sheets of paper used for official documents. They are cube-shaped, white and full of little holes, like a honeycomb or a small wasp's nest. This volcano is known as 'the Sicilian volcano'. On the same island is to be found the tomb of Porphyry the Wise, the author of the *Isagogus* or *Introduction to the Science of Logic* – the book and the man are both well known.

I have written on all the volcanoes of the world, such as that of Wadi Barahūt in the Hadramaut and the land of al-Shihr; the volcano of Zābaj in the Sea of China; and the volcano in the land of Asak, which lies between Fars and the Ahwaz, in the governorship of

Arrajān, which is a part of Fars. The fires of this last volcano can be seen at night from a distance of some 20 *farsakhs* [a *farsakh* is about 3 miles] and they are famous throughout the Muslim world.

The word *atma* ('volcano') actually means a source of fire rising up from the ground.

I found in a book which came into my hands in Fustāt in Egypt in the year 336/947, presented by God-mar, bishop of Gerona, one of the cities of the Franks, to al-Hakam, the heir apparent to his father ʿAbd al-Rahmān, ruler of al-Andalus at this time, referred to in his dominions by the title 'Commander of the Faithful', that the first king of the Franks was Clovis, and that he was a pagan converted to Christianity by his wife Clotilde.

7. *The Lombards*

We have already mentioned that the Lombards are descended from Japhet, the son of Noah. Their country extends to the west, but their homeland lies to the north. They possess many islands inhabited by various ethnic groups. They themselves are strong and power-ful and very hard to subdue. They have many cities and are united under a single king. Their kings are always called *adākīs* [dukes].

The largest of all their cities and the seat of their kingdom is Benevento. A great river crosses the city and divides it into two principal quarters. This river is one of the most considerable in the world and one of the most wonderful. It is called Sabato. It is mentioned by numerous earlier writers who have dealt with the subject.

The Muslims in al-Andalus and the Maghrib, who were neighbours of the Lombards, took a number of towns from them by force – Bari, Taranto, the city of Sardinia and other large cities – and occupied them for a time. Then the Lombards took courage once again and counter-attacked, casting out the Muslims after a long series of battles. At the present day, 336/947, the towns which we have mentioned above are once more in the hands of the Lombards.

The Galicians, Franks, Slavs, Lombards and other peoples we have mentioned above live in lands which all adjoin one another. Most of these peoples are currently in a state of war with the inhabitants of al-Andalus.

The ruler of this last country is, in our day, a very redoubtable and powerful ruler ['Abd al-Rahmān III]. 'Abd al-Rahmān ibn Mu'awiya ibn Hishām ['Abd al-Rahmān I, 756–88] went to al-Andalus at the beginning of the 'Abbasid dynasty, and the story of how he reached that country is filled with remarkable incidents.

The capital of al-Andalus is Córdoba, as we have mentioned above. The Muslims possess many towns, and their cultivated lands extend without interruption over a vast area, all the way to the frontier towns along all the borders of their territory. They have repeatedly seen the neighbouring nations, descendants of Japhet, join forces against them – the Galicians, Burgundians, Franks and others. The present ruler of al-Andalus ['Abd al-Rahmān III], who is very powerful, can mount

100,000 men, to say nothing of foot soldiers, baggage animals and equipment. God alone is Eternal!

8. *The Norsemen*

Sometime before the year 300/912–13, ships carrying thousands of men reached al-Andalus by sea and raided the Atlantic coasts. The people of al-Andalus claimed that these enemies were one of the nations of the Majūs [Vikings], who came to attack them by sea every two hundred years, and that they reach their country by means of a strait which communicates with the Atlantic Ocean. This is not to be confused with the strait upon which is the bronze lighthouse [the Strait of Gibraltar]. Personally, I think – but God best knows the truth – that this strait communicates with the Sea of Azov and the Sea of Pontus [Black Sea] and that the attackers were those Rūs we have already mentioned, since they are the only people who sail those seas that communicate with the Atlantic Ocean.

9. *The Slavs*

The Slavs are descended from Mādhāy, the son of Japhet, the son of Noah, and all the Slavic peoples derive their origins and trace their genealogies back to him, or at least this is the opinion of most of those who have devoted themselves to the question. They dwell in the north, whence they have spread westwards.

The Slavs are divided into several different peoples who war among themselves and have kings. Some of them belong to the Christian faith, being of the Jacobite sect, while the others are pagans and have no scripture and know nothing of divine law.

Among the different peoples who make up this pagan race, there is one that in ancient times held sovereign power. Their king was called Mājik, and they themselves were known as Walītābā [Wiltzes?]. In the past, all the Slavs recognized their superiority, because it was from among them that they chose the paramount ruler, and all the other chieftains considered themselves his vassals.

Among the Slavic peoples of the second rank should be mentioned in the following order: the Istrāna, whose king in our own times is called Basqlābij [Vasclav?]; then the Dūlāba [western Dulebians?], whose present king is called Wānjslāf. Next are the Namjīn [Niemczyn, 'Germans'], whose king is called Gharānd [Conrad]; among all the Slavs these are the bravest and the best horsemen. After, come the Manābin, whose king is called Ratīmīr; the Sarbīn [the Serbs], a Slavic people much feared for reasons that it would take too long to explain and whose deeds would need much too detailed an account. They have no particular religious affiliation.

Then there is the people called the Murāwa [the Moravians] and another known as the Kharwātīn [the Croats], and yet another called the Sāsīn [either the Saxons or the Czech 'Cacin'], then the Khashānīn and the Barānijābīn. The names of some of their kings which we have given are in fact dynastic titles.

The Sarbīn, whom we have just mentioned, have the custom of burning themselves alive when a king or chieftain dies. They also immolate his horses. These people have customs similar to those of the Indians.

In the land of the Khazars there are, as well as the Khazars themselves, a Slav and a Rūs population and that these last also burn themselves. These Slavs and other related peoples extend to the east rather than to the west.

The foremost of the Slav kings is the ruler of Aldayr, whose domains include great cities and much cultivated land, vast troops and countless armies. Muslim merchants make their way to his capital with all kinds of merchandise.

After this, on the borders of this Slavic king, comes the king of al-Afragh [Prague], who has a gold mine, towns, extensive well-cultivated lands, numerous soldiers and a large population. He is at war with the Byzantines, the Franks, the Bazkard [the Magyars] and other nations besides; the hostilities among them are continuous.

Neighbouring this Slavic king is the king of the Turks. These people are the handsomest, the most numerous and the most warlike of all. The Slavs comprise many different peoples and are very far-flung, but this work is not the place for a detailed description and classification of them.

I began by mentioning the king whose suzerainty has been recognized by all the other rulers since ancient times, that is to say Mājik, king of the Walītābā, who are the original, pure-blooded Slavs, the most highly honoured and take precedence over all the other branches of the race.

Later, dissent having established itself among these peoples, their original organization was destroyed and the various families formed isolated groups, each choosing a king, as we have said above. An account of all these events would take too long, all the more so since I have already related them in a general way and with great detail in my earlier works, the *Historical Annals* and the *Intermediate History*.

10. *Viking raiders*

The Rūs [Vikings who were established on the Russian river systems] are many nations, divided into different groups. One of them, the most numerous, is the al-Ludh'āna. They separate and travel far and wide, trading with al-Andalus, Rome, Constantinople and the Khazars. It was just after the year 300/912–13 that some five hundred of their ships, each manned by a hundred men, entered the Strait of Pontus, which joins the river of the Khazars [the Volga]. Men are posted there by the king of the Khazars, and from their well-fortified positions they are under orders to bar the way to anyone coming from the Sea of Pontus or by land adjoining any branch of the river of the Khazars that communicates with the Sea of Pontus.

This is because the nomadic Ghuzz [Oguz] Turks set up their winter camps in these parts. As the water courses that link the river of the Khazars with the Strait of Pontus are often frozen, the Ghuzz cross them with their horses, for there is so much water and it is frozen so solid that there is no danger of it breaking under their weight, and thus they raid into the land of the Khazars. On several occasions, the guards having failed to repel them, the king of the Khazars has been compelled to march out against them in force, so as to prevent them from crossing the ice, and thus he has saved his kingdom from invasion. In summer, there is no way the Turks would be able to cross.

When the Rūs vessels reached the Khazar checkpoint that guards the entrance to the strait, they sent to ask the king for permission to cross his kingdom and make their way down the river of the Khazars and so enter the Khazar Sea [the Caspian Sea], which is also known by the names of the barbarian peoples who live by it – the Sea of Jurjān, the Sea of Tabaristān, and so forth. The Rūs contracted to give the king half of anything they managed to pillage from the people along the shores of that sea. The ruler agreed to their request, and they entered the strait and reached the mouth of the river [the Don], continuing upstream until they reached the river of the Khazars. Then they went down that river, passed through the city of Itil, and at last arrived at its mouth, where it flows into the Khazar Sea. The river of the Khazars is wide and the volume of water it carries very great. The Rūs ships spread out across this sea. Raiding parties then rode against Jīl [Gilan], Daylam, Tabaristān and Ābaskūn on the coast of Jurjān. They invaded the lands of

Naphtha [Bākū] and harried as far as Azerbaijān – indeed, the city of Ardabīl in Azerbaijān is three days' journey from the sea.

The Rūs spilled rivers of blood, seized women and children and property, raided, and everywhere destroyed and burned. The people who lived on these shores were in turmoil, for they had never been attacked by an enemy from the sea, and their shores had been visited only by the ships of merchants and fishermen. Fighting ceaselessly with the people of Jīl, Daylam, the Jurjān coast, the frontier region of Bardha'a, Arrān, Baylaqān and Azerbaijān, and also against a general sent by Ibn Abī al-Sāj, the Rūs pushed on to the Naphtha Coast, which is known by the name of Bākū and forms part of the kingdom of Shirwān.

On returning from these expeditions, they took refuge among the islands only a few miles off the Naphtha Coast. At that time, 'Ali ibn al-Haytham was king of Shirwān. Troops were marshalled. They embarked on boats and merchant ships and set out for these islands. But the Rūs turned on them, and thousands of Muslims were killed or drowned. The Rūs stayed many months doing the deeds we have described without any of the peoples who live around this sea being able to oppose them. The inhabitants of these shores, which are very densely populated, did what they could to prepare themselves and remained in a state of high alert.

Gorged with loot and worn out by raiding, the Rūs returned to the mouth of the Khazar River and sent a message to the king of the Khazars together with the share of the spoils they had promised him. This prince has no ships and his subjects are not familiar with the art of navigation, otherwise it would be a calamity for the Muslims.

Meanwhile, the Arsiyya and other Muslims who live in the lands of the Khazars learned what had happened and said to the Khazar, 'Let us do what we want to these people who have sacked the lands of our Muslim brothers, spilt their blood and dragged their women and children away into slavery.'

The king was unable to stop them, so he sent to the Rūs and warned them that the Muslims had decided to attack them. The Muslims gathered an army and went out to meet the Rūs going downstream. When the two armies were within sight of each other, the Rūs left their boats. The Muslims numbered about 15,000; they had horses and were well equipped, and they were accompanied by a certain number of Christians resident in Itil.

The two sides fought for at least three days, and God gave the victory to the Muslims. The Rūs were put to the sword or drowned. The number killed on the banks of the Khazar River numbered 30,000. Some 5000 managed to escape and crossed to the other side with their boats to Burtās [a branch of the Volga], or else abandoned their boats and entrusted themselves to dry land. Some of them were killed by the inhabitants of Burtās; others reached the Muslim Bulghārs, who massacred them. Some 30,000 were thus slain on the banks of the Khazar River. Since that year, the Rūs have never tried anything of the kind again.

11. The Khazars

The king, his court and all those of the Khazar race practice Judaism, to which the king of the Khazars was converted during the reign of Harūn al-Rashīd. Many Jews from Muslim and Byzantine cities came to settle among the Khazars, particularly since Romanus I, the king of the Byzantines in our own time, 332/943, forced the Jews in his kingdom to convert to Christianity. Further on in this volume we shall give the history of the rulers of Byzantium, which we shall set out in order, and shall speak of this king as well as the two other rulers who shared power with him. A great number of Jews therefore fled from the land of the Byzantines and sought refuge with the Khazars. This is not the place to speak of the conversion of the Khazar ruler to Judaism, as we have already discussed this subject in our previous works.

The pagans who live in this country belong to many different races, among which are the Slavs and the Rūs, who live in one of the two parts of the city. They burn their dead on pyres along with the deceased's horses, arms and equipment. When a man dies, his wife is burned alive with him, but if the wife dies before her husband, the man does not suffer the same fate. If a man dies before marriage, he is given a posthumous wife. The women passionately want to be burned because they believe they will enter paradise. This is a custom, as we have already mentioned, that is current in India but with this difference: there, the woman is not burned unless she gives her consent.

The Muslims are dominant in the land of the Khazars because they make up the king's army. They are known by the name Arsiyya. They originally came from the region around Khwārizm, and settled in the Khazar kingdom a long time ago, shortly after the appearance of Islam, when they fled the double ravages of famine and plague that devastated their homeland. These are strong, courageous men, in whom the king of the Khazars places his confidence in the wars which he wages. When they established themselves in his kingdom they stipulated, among other things, that they be allowed the free exercise of their religion, that they might have mosques and publicly give the call to prayer, and that the king's chief minister should be chosen from among their number. In our days the one who occupies this post is a Muslim named Ahmad ibn Kūyah. He has made an agreement with the king whereby he and his army will not fight against Muslims, but will march into battle against the infidel. Today, around 7000 of them serve as the king's mounted archers. They carry a shield and wear helmets and chain mail. They also have lancers equipped and armed like other Muslim soldiers.

They also have their own *qadīs*. It is a rigid custom in the Khazar capital that there should be seven judges: two for the Muslims; two for the Khazars, who make their decisions in accordance with the Torah; two for the Christians, who make theirs according to the Gospels; and one for the Slavs, Rūs and other pagans.

This latter judge follows pagan law, which is the product of natural reason. When a serious case comes up that the judges cannot decide, the parties involved consult the Muslim *qadīs* and obey the decision made in accordance with Islamic law. The king of the Khazars is the only ruler of these eastern countries to have a paid army. All the Muslims who live in the country are known as Arsiyya.

The Rūs and the Slavs, who are pagans as we have said, served as mercenaries and slaves of the king. Besides the Arsiyya there are a certain number of Muslim merchants and artisans who have emigrated to this country because of the justice and security with which the king rules. In addition to the congregational mosque, whose minaret towers over the king's palace, there are many other mosques to which are attached schools where the Qur'ān is taught to children. If the Muslims and the Christians united, the king would have no power over them.

12. The Bulghārs

The Khazars have ships which they sail on a river which flows, above their city, into the great river which traverses it [the Volga and its tributaries]. This river is called the Burtās, and its banks are inhabited by many sedentary Turkish peoples who form part of the Khazar kingdom. Their settlements are continuous and extend from the land of the Khazars to the land of the Bulghārs. This river, which flows from the land of the

23

Bulghārs, carries vessels from both kingdoms. Burtās, as we have already said, is also the name of a Turkish people who live along the banks of this river, from which they have taken their name. The pelts of black and red foxes called *burtāsī* are exported from their country. Some of these furs, above all the black, are worth 100 dinars or more. The red furs are worth less. The black furs are worn by the Arab and non-Arab kings, who esteem them more than they do sable, ermine and other similar furs. They make hats, kaftans and fur coats out of them. There is no king who does not possess a fur coat or a kaftan lined with the black fox fur of Burtās.

The upper reaches of the Khazar River communicate by one of its branches with a gulf of the Sea of Pontus, also called the 'Sea of the Rūs' because the Rūs, who are the only ones to sail it, live on one of its shores. They form a numerous pagan nation that doesn't recognize authority or revealed law. Many of their merchants trade with the Bulghārs. In their country the Rūs have a silver mine comparable to the one in the mountain of Banjhīr in Khurasan.

The Bulghār capital is located on the Sea of Pontus. If I am not mistaken, these peoples, who are a kind of Turk, inhabit the seventh clime [*iqlīm*; geographers divided the world for mapping purposes into seven 'climes', or regions]. Caravans continually pass back and forth between the Bulghārs and Khwarizm, which is a dependency of the kingdom of Khurasan. Because the route passes through the encampments of other Turkish nomads, they are constrained to place themselves under their protection. At the present moment, 332/943, the king of the Bulghārs is a Muslim, converted as the result of a dream during the caliphate of Muqtadir [908–32], sometime after the year 310/922. One of his sons has made the pilgrimage to Mecca, and when he passed through Baghdād the caliph gave him a standard, a black robe of honour and a gift of money. This people have a congregational mosque.

Their king invaded the territories of Constantinople at the head of at least 50,000 cavalry. From there he dispatched expeditions which reached all the way to Rome, then to Spain, the territories of the Burgundians, Galicians and the Franks. In order to reach Constantinople, this king had to travel for two months along a route which passed through both cultivated and desert lands. In 312/924 a Muslim expedition set out from Tarsus on the Syrian frontier under the command of the eunuch Thamal, known as al-Dulafī, commander of the frontier. He was admiral of a fleet made up of vessels from Syria and Basra. After having crossed the mouth of the channel that leads to Constantinople and then another gulf [the Adriatic] of the Mediterranean, which has no outlet, the Muslims reached Venice. A detachment of Bulghārs who had travelled overland joined them to reinforce them and told them that their king was a short distance away. This proves the truth of our statement that some units of the Bulgarian cavalry reached the Mediterranean coast. A number of them embarked on the ships from Tarsus and returned with them.

The Bulghārs are a large, powerful and warlike

nation which has subjugated all the neighbouring peoples. One of the Bulghār cavalrymen who had embraced Islam along with their king held off one or even two hundred infidel horsemen. It is only thanks to their defensive walls that the inhabitants of Constantinople are able to resist them. It is the same with all those who live in this country: the only way they can defend themselves from the attacks of these formidable enemies is by fortresses and defensive walls.

13. *Land of the midnight sun*

In the land of the Bulghārs the nights are extremely short during part of the year. They even say that between nightfall and dawn a man barely has time to bring his cooking pot to the boil. In our previous works we have explained this phenomenon from the astronomical point of view and have shown why, at a point on the earth in the Polar Regions, there are six consecutive months of darkness, succeeded by six months of daylight. The scientific explanation for this is given by the astronomers in their astronomical tables.

14. *The iron gates*

The Caucasus is a great chain of mountains. This huge area contains a large number of kingdoms and peoples. There are no less than seventy-two different peoples, each with their own king and speaking a language different from their neighbours. The mountains are seamed with valleys and ravines. At the head of one of these passes is the city of Derbend, built by Chosroe Anushīrwān [Sasanian ruler of Iran, 531–79] in a place between the mountains and the Sea of the Khazars [the Caspian Sea]. The same ruler built the wall, one end of which extends for a mile into the sea and the other reaches into the Caucasus, following the rise and fall of the mountain crests and descending into the valleys for a distance of some 40 farsakhs until it terminates at a fortified point called Tabarsarān. Every three miles or so, depending on the importance of the route upon which it opens, he placed an iron gate; nearby, inside the walls, guards were stationed to protect and watch that portion of the wall. This rampart formed an impassable barrier against the evil intentions of the peoples inhabiting the mountains: the Khazars, Alans, various Turkish peoples, Avars and other infidel tribes.

The high peaks of the Caucasus cover such a large area that it would take two months or more to traverse their length or breadth. Only the Creator can number the peoples that live there. One of the passes through these mountains, near Derbend, leads to the Sea of the Khazars, as we have said. Another leads to the Black Sea, into which flows the channel of Constantinople. Trebizond is located on this sea. Every year many markets are held there, frequented by a large number of Muslim, Byzantine, Armenian and other merchants, without counting those who come from Circassia.

If God, Mighty and Exalted, had not, in His wisdom

and great power and compassion for the perilous situation of His servants, aided the rulers of Iran in founding the city of Derbend and constructing these ramparts, which extend both into the sea and over the mountains as we have said, and in building castles and establishing colonies ruled by properly constituted kings, there is no doubt that the rulers of Georgia, the Alans, the Avars, the Turks and other nations we have named would have invaded the territories of Bardha'a, Arrān, Baylaqān, Azerbaijān, Zanjān, Abhār, Qazwīn, Hamadān, Dīnawar, Nihāwand and the frontiers of the dependencies of Kufa and Basra, thereby reaching Iraq, had God not blocked their advance in the way we have described.

This is especially true now that Islam has weakened and declined. The Byzantines are making inroads against the Muslims, the Pilgrimage is in peril, Holy War has ceased, communications have been interrupted and roads are insecure. Every local military chief has taken power in his region and made himself independent, just as the 'party kings' did after the death of Alexander the Great, until Ardashīr ibn Bābak, the Sasanian, re-established political unity and put an end to endemic warfare, restoring security to the people and cultivation to the land. This lasted until Muhammad, May Prayers and Peace Be Upon Him, received his mission from God and effaced the vestiges of unbelief and the traces of other doctrines. Islam has always been triumphant, until this year 332/943, when under the caliphate of the Commander of the Faithful Muttaqī [the Caliph Muttaqī, 940–44], its supports are shaking and its foundations crumbling. We seek help from God for the state we find ourselves in.

15. *The Alans*

The kingdom of the Alans borders on the Avars and its king is called *Karkundāj*, which is the general title for all its rulers, just as those of the Avars are called *Fīlān-Shāh*. The capital of the kingdom of the Alans is called Maghas – a word which means 'flies'. In this country too there are castles and pleasure gardens outside the towns, where the king goes from time to time. The king of the Alans and the ruler of the Avars have very recently made an agreement to give each other their sisters in marriage.

After the appearance of Islam, during the 'Abbasid dynasty, the rulers of the Alans, who had been pagans, converted to Christianity, but after the year 320/931 they foreswore their new beliefs and chased out the bishops and priests sent to them by the Byzantine emperor.

Between the kingdom of the Alans and the Caucasus there is a castle and a bridge built over a great river. The castle is called the Gate of the Alans and it was built in times long past by one of the ancient rulers of Persia, Isfandyār ibn Bistāsf. He stationed a garrison there to prevent the Alans from reaching the Caucasus. There was no other way, except by this bridge, protected by this castle, that they could get there. The castle was built on an impregnable rock and could not be taken or even approached without the permission of those who held it. Inside the castle, on the rock upon which it was built, a spring of fresh water rose. This is one of the most famous castles in the world for its unconquerable position. The Persian poets often mention it and tell the story of its building by Isfandyār ibn Bistāsf.

Isfandyār fought many wars against the different peoples of the east. He penetrated to the farthest reaches of the lands of the Turks and destroyed the city of Sufr – the City of Brass – a place almost impossible to reach and so positioned as to seem to defy attack; its strength has become proverbial among the Persians.

These exploits of Isfandyār, which we have just mentioned, are told in full detail in the work entitled *Kitāb al-Baykār*, which has been translated into Arabic by Ibn al-Muqaffa'.

When Maslama ibn 'Abd al-Malik ibn Marwān [son of the Umayyad Caliph 'Abd al-Malik, 685–705] reached this region and had reduced the inhabitants to submission, he stationed an Arab garrison in the castle, and their descendants continue to hold this vital post. Most of the time they receive their provisions overland from Tiflis, which is five days' march away. A single man in this castle could bar the way to all the kings of the infidels, thanks to its position, almost hanging suspended in the air, commanding at one and the same time road, bridge and river gorge.

The king of the Alans can put 30,000 horsemen into the field. He is a powerful king, strong and highly respected among kings. His lands are so densely populated, the houses so close together, that the cocks call to each other from village to village, which are almost contiguous throughout the country.

In the neighbourhood of the Alans, between the Caucasus and the Mediterranean, are to be found the Kashak [Circassians]. They are a specific ethnic group, following the Zoroastrian religion. Among the nations we have mentioned as inhabiting this region there is not one which produces a more perfect physical type, fairer complexion, handsomer men or more pleasing women. No people are taller, with slimmer waists and hips, more shapely buttocks, or with better-proportioned figures.

The women are famous for the delights they bring to the bedchamber. They wear white dresses and over them brocades from Byzantium, or scarlet cloth, or other materials worked with gold. In this country a linen cloth called *talā* is made, finer and more closely woven than the kind known as *dabīqī*, and a piece of clothing in this material costs ten dinars. It is exported to the neighbouring Islamic lands. Their neighbours also export this material, but it cannot compare with that produced by the Kashaks.

The Alans dominate this people, who can withstand them only because they have fortresses along the coast to protect them. This sea, over which there is a certain disagreement, is considered by some to be the Mediterranean, while according to others it is the Sea of Pontus. In any case, the Kashaks are close by sea to Trebizond, and merchandise from this city is brought to them by ship, and they in turn send goods there. Their weakness compared with the Alans comes of their not being united under one rule. It is certain that if all those who spoke their language formed a single closely united nation, neither the Alans nor any other race would be able to do anything against them. Their name is Persian and means 'pride, boasting'. Indeed, among the Persians the word *kash* is applied to an arrogant, vainglorious man.

On the shores of the same sea, and near the Kashaks, live another people whose territory is called *al-Saba' Buldān*, 'The Seven Countries'. They form a powerful nation, well able to enforce respect, and their authority extends over a wide area. I do not know what ethnic group they form, and no one has been able to inform me of their religion.

Next, one comes to a very numerous people, whose lands are separated from those of the Kashaks by a river as great as the Euphrates, which flows into the Sea of Pontus, on the shores of which stands Trebizond. This people is called Iram, and is a very strange-looking race and is pagan. It is said that a peculiar thing happens along these shores. Every year, a fish comes and places itself at the disposal of the inhabitants, who cut off a piece. Later, it comes back a second time and offers them another part of its body, which they slice off; new flesh has already replaced that which was removed the first time. This fact is well known to all the infidels who live in these lands.

16. Jewish scholars and the Bible

The translation of the Bible from Hebrew into Greek was done by seventy-two learned men at Alexandria in Egypt. This text has been translated into Arabic by many scholars, ancient and modern, among them Hunayn ibn Ishāq [809–73, a Nestorian scholar – the most important of the early translators of Greek scientific texts into Arabic]. It is commonly considered the most accurate recension of the Bible.

The Jews, both those called the Ashma'at [Rabbinical Jews], who form the great majority of the nation, and the Ananites [the non-Rabbinical Jews], who all profess the doctrines of justice and the unity of God, use it as a commentary on the Hebrew text of the Torah, the Prophets and the Psalms – in all, twenty-four books. This translation is held in great esteem by them. I have met many of their scholars, including Abū Kathīr Yahyā ibn Zakariyā, the Scribe of Tiberias, who belonged to the sect of the Ashma'at and died towards the year 320/932; and Sa'īd ibn Ya 'qūb al-Fayyūmī, also of the sect of the Ashma'at and a disciple of Abū Kathīr, whose translation is the most esteemed by his co-religionists. He came into conflict in Iraq with the exilarch Da'ūd ibn Zakka, a descendant of David, during the caliphate of Muqtadir [908–32]. This conflict caused turmoil among the Jews. He was summoned to the presence of the vizier 'Alī ibn 'Īsā and other ministers, *qadīs* and men of learning in order to iron out the disputes among the Jews. A large party of them had chosen al-Fayyūmī as their leader, and obeyed him. He died in the year 330/942. Da'ūd, called al-Qūmīsī, who died in Jerusalem in 334/946, is numbered among these learned men, as well as Ibrāhīm al-Baghdādī. I never met either man. I did have numerous conversations in Palestine and Jordan with Abū Kathīr; we discussed the abrogation of laws, the difference between law and works and other subjects. I also held discussions with Yahūdha ibn Yūsuf, known as Ibn Abī al-Thanā, a student of Thābit ibn Qurra the Sabian [826–901, the leading scientist and mathematician of the tenth century, and a prolific translator from Greek into Syriac and Arabic], on philosophy and medicine at Raqqa in the province of Diyār Mudar; and with Sa'īd ibn 'Ali, known as Ibn Ishlamīyā, also at Raqqa. I also met many of their theologians at Baghdād, men such as Ya'qūb ibn Mardawayh and Yūsuf ibn Qayūmā. The last of these men that I met, some time after the year 300/913, was Ibrāhīm al-Yahūdhī al-Tustārī. He had the subtlest mind and was the most versed in speculative questions of the learned men of recent times.

17. The journey of the Three Magi

King Cyrus, who reigned at the time the Messiah was born, sent him three messengers [King Cyrus was not the ruler of Persia at the time of Christ's birth]. He gave one of them a bag of frankincense, the second a bag of myrrh, and to the third a bag of gold dust. Their way was guided by a star the king described to them. They journeyed until they reached Syria and finally came to the Messiah and His mother Mary. The Christians embroider the story of these men, but it is found in the Gospels. Thus it is said that King Cyrus saw the star, which rose at the time of the birth of the Messiah, and that it moved along while the king's messengers were travelling and halted when they halted, and so on. All this can be found in greater detail in our *Historical Annals*, where we have set down both the Persian and the Christian versions of this legend. There can be read the story of the two loaves Mary gave them and what happened when they hid them under a rock, and how these loaves sank into the depths of the earth in the province of Fars, and how wells were dug at the site and two flames of fire burst out and shone above the surface of the earth.

18. The Empress Helena and the Invention of the True Cross

After the death of Diocletian, Constantine became the ruler of Rome [Constantine I the Great, 306–37]. He worshipped idols. He was the first of the Roman kings to move his capital from Rome to Byzantium, that is, to Constantinople. He built this city and gave it his name, by which it is still known today. While he was founding Constantinople and under threat of an attack by the Sasanian ruler of Persia, he entered into relations with the barbarians, the full story of which would be of some interest. After having been on the throne for a year, he left Rome and became a Christian. His mother Helena visited Syria and founded many churches, then went to Jerusalem and discovered the cross upon which, according to the Christians, the Messiah had been crucified. Once she had it, she covered it with gold and silver and commemorated the discovery by a feast day called the Feast of the Cross, which falls on 14 September. It is on this day that in Egypt the dykes and canals are opened, as we shall explain further on in the chapter devoted to the description of Egypt.

The same queen built the church in Emesa [modern Homs] which rests upon four pillars and is one of the most marvellous buildings in the world. She dug up the riches and treasures hidden in Egypt and Syria and used them to found churches and strengthen the Christian faith. All the churches of Syria, Egypt and the land of Byzantium owe their origin to this Queen Helena, the mother of Constantine. Her name is written on the cross of each church she built. The letter *h* does not exist in the Greek alphabet, so the name 'Helena' is composed of only five letters. The first corresponds to our long *a*, pronounced as if it were *e*; its numerical value is 5. The second letter is *l*, with the value of 30; the third is another long *a*, pronounced like an *e*, again with the value of 5; the fourth is an *n*, with the value of 50; and the fifth is a *y*, with the value of 10. So the letters all add up to make 100. This is what the word representing the value of 100 looks like in the Greek alphabet: Ελένη.

19. Constantine's vision of the cross

This is how Constantine, the son of Helena, entered into the Christian faith. He had gone out to fight a war with the Burjān [the Goths] or some other nation, and the fighting between them had gone on for almost a year. Then things began to turn against him. A large part of his army was killed, and he feared defeat. Then he saw in a dream lances decorated with banners and flags descend from heaven; at their tips were crosses of gold, silver, iron, copper and different kinds of precious stones. A voice said, 'Take these spears and fight your enemies and you will prevail!' In his dream he took up these arms against his enemies, and thanks to their help defeated them and put them to flight. When he awoke, he ordered the sign he had seen in his dream fastened to the ends of lances, which were carried before his army. He attacked the enemy army, defeated it and put it to the sword. He then returned to Nicaea and asked men who were well informed if such a sign existed in any religion or sect. He learned that the sect that had adopted this sign gathered in Jerusalem in Syria, and was told of the persecutions it had undergone under the kings who had preceded him. He immediately sent messengers to Syria, in particular to Jerusalem, summoning 318 bishops to join him at Nicaea. He told them what had happened, and they instructed him in the doctrines of the Christian religion. Such was the aim of the first Synod, or as we shall explain, the first council. Others believe that

Helena, his mother, had already embraced Christianity, but hid her faith from her son until the moment he had his dream.

20. *The Church of the Virgin at Nazareth*

When Mary, the daughter of Amram, was seventeen years old, God sent Gabriel who breathed the Holy Spirit into her and she became pregnant with the Messiah, Jesus, May Peace Be Upon Him! Jesus was born in a village called Bethlehem, a few miles from Jerusalem, on Wednesday, 24 December. His history is recounted by God in His book, in clear words by the tongue of His Prophet Muhammad, May Prayers and Peace Be Upon Him! The Christians claim that Jesus of Nazareth, that is the Messiah, followed the religion of His ancestors and studied the Torah and other ancient writings for thirty, or it is said, twenty-nine years in a synagogue called al-Midras in the city of Tiberias, in the region of Jordan. One day, while reading the Book of Isaiah, He saw these words traced in letters of light: 'You are My son, the particular object of My affection; I have chosen you for My soul.' He closed the book and returned it to a servant of the synagogue, saying, 'Now the word of God is fulfilled in the son of man.' It is said that the Messiah lived in a village called Nazareth in the territory of al-Lajjūn in the district of Jordan, and it is from this village that the Christians take their name of 'Nazarenes'.

I visited a church in this village which is held in great

veneration by the Christians. In it are stone sarcophagi containing the bones of the dead from which runs an oil thick as syrup. The Christians anoint themselves with it to receive its blessing. When the Messiah passed by Lake Tiberias, He saw some fishermen, the sons of Zebedee, and twelve fullers. He called upon them to follow God, saying, 'Follow me, and fish for men.' Three of the fishermen, the sons of Zebedee, and all twelve fullers followed Him.

Matthew, John, Mark and Luke are the four apostles who have transmitted the Gospels in which they have written the history of the Messiah, His birth, the way in which He received baptism from John, son of Zacharia, that is, John the Baptist, in Lake Tiberias – or according to others, in the River Jordan, a river that issues forth from Lake Tiberias and runs towards the Dead Sea. They recount the wonders and miracles He performed, the treatment He received from the Jews, until the time, when He was thirty-three years old, that Almighty God lifted Him up to heaven. The Gospels give extensive information about the Messiah, Mary and Joseph the Carpenter, but we shall pass over them in silence, for neither Almighty God nor His Prophet Muhammad, May Prayers and Peace Be Upon Him, speaks of them.

21. *The decline of Greek science*

From the days of the ancient Greeks through early Byzantine times, scientific knowledge continued to grow and develop. Learned men and philosophers were held in great esteem, and investigated the natural world, the human body, reason and the soul, as well as the *quadrivium*: that is, arithmetic, the science of numbers; geometry, the study of space and figures; astronomy, the science of heavenly bodies, and music, which is the science of ordering sounds.

The sciences were financially supported, honoured everywhere, universally pursued; they were like tall edifices supported by strong foundations. Then the Christian religion appeared in Byzantium and the centres of learning were eliminated, their vestiges effaced and the edifice of Greek learning was obliterated. Everything the ancient Greeks had brought to light vanished, and the discoveries of the ancients were altered out of recognition.

22. Christian historians

A large number of Christians – Melkites, Nestorians and Jacobites – of all periods have written historical works. The best I have seen by Melkite authors on the history of kings, prophets, peoples and countries are: the book of Maḥbūb, son of Constantine, of Manbij; and the book of Sa'īd ibn Bitrīq [877–940, the earliest Christian Arab historian], known as Ibn al-Faraj, the Egyptian, Patriarch of the See of Mark at Alexandria. I met this author in Fustāt. His history ends with the caliphate of Rādī [934–40]. Another Melkite historian is the Egyptian monk Athenius, whose book covers the history of the Byzantine rulers and other nations and recounts all that concerns the history of the Christians from the time of Adam to that of Constantine, son of Helena. I saw a book in the hands of the Nestorians of the east by the scribe Yaʿqūb ibn Zakarīyā of Kaskar. I also saw copies in Iraq and Syria. It includes learned remarks on these matters and other information of a similar nature on Christian affairs. The Jacobites also have a book which deals with the Byzantine rulers, the ancient Greeks, and the lives and actions of their philosophers; it was written by Abū Zakarīyā Dankhā, the Christian. This author was powerful and subtle in disputation. I had numerous discussions with him on the Trinity and other dogmas in the Umm Jaʿfar quarter of Baghdād, in the western part of the city, and in Takrit, in the Green Church, in the year 313/926. I have spoken of these in the book *Questions and Causes on Doctrines and Creeds* and in the book *The Secret of Life*.

23. *The transmission of Greek science*

Aristotle was the student of Plato, Plato of Socrates and Socrates of Archelaus, whom he followed for the natural sciences, but not for the other sciences. The name Archelaus means 'head of wild beasts'. Archelaus was the pupil of Anaxagoras. In our book *On the Different Sorts of Knowledge and the Events of Past Ages* we spoke of philosophy and its definition, of the number of topics into which it is divided, and the views of Pythagoras, Thales of Miletus, the Stoics, Plato, Aristotle and others, and the definitions they have given to the word and the qualities which distinguish the true philosopher, his way of life, comportment, manners and dress. We described the categories of philosophies, how they were established, the methods of teaching philosophy down to the present day and its goals. We explained the aim of treatises on logic, their composition, why they were written and the use to which they can be put, as well as why they are composed in eight books and what the aim of each book is, and above all how the reader who proposes to read one of these treatises on logic should proceed. We have shown in which branch of art the craft of philosophy should be placed, the number of different definitions that have been given to it, and how these definitions were arrived at, and what they mean. We described the number of divisions of both early and later philosophy, how these divisions were arrived at and why they have prevailed, and why political philosophy, which takes its point of departure from Socrates, passed from him to Plato, then to Aristotle, from Aristotle to his nephew Theophrastus, and finally to Eudemus and those who came after him, one after another.

We described how the Academy was transferred from Athens to Alexandria in Egypt, and how the Emperor Augustus, after having killed Cleopatra, founded two centres of learning, Alexandria and Rome. Theodosius, the king who ruled during the time of the People of the Cave [the 'Seven Sleepers of Ephesus'], moved the Academy from Rome back to Alexandria.

We have also explained why, in the days of 'Umar ibn 'Abd al-'Azīz [the Ummayad caliph 'Umar II, 717–20], it was moved to Antioch, and then to Harrān in the days of Mutawakkil [the 'Abbasid caliph Mutawakkil, 847–61].

Its work was continued under Mu'tadid [the 'Abbasid caliph Mu'tadid, 892–902] by Quwayri and Yūhannā ibn Haylān, who died in Baghdād during the caliphate of Muqtadir, and Ibrāhīm of Merv, then Abū Muhammad ibn Karnīb and Abū Bishr Mattā ibn Yūnis, both pupils of Ibrāhīm of Merv. In our day the commentary of Mattā ibn Yūnis on the logic of Aristotle is considered authoritative; he died during the caliphate of Rādī. The torch was then passed to Abū Nasr Muhammad ibn Muhammad al-Farābī, the student of Yūhannā ibn Haylān, who died in Damascus in the month of Rajab 339/950. I know no one today as learned as he, except one man, a Christian living in Baghdād, known as Abū Zakarīyā ibn 'Adī, whose point of departure, opinions and method are those of Muhammad ibn Zakarīyā al-Rāzī [c.854–c.925]; this system is that of the Pythagoreans with regard to the 'first philosophy', as we have explained previously.

24. Persepolis

The Persians have a fire temple revered by the Mazdaeans in Istakhr [ancient Persepolis] in Fars. In ancient times it was filled with idols; they were removed by Humāy, daughter of Bahman ibn Isfandīyār, who transformed it into a fire temple. Later the fire was removed, and the structure fell into ruins. Today, in the year 336/947, they claim that it is the mosque of Solomon, son of David, so it is known as the Masjid Sulaymān. It is located about a farsakh from the city of Istakhr. I visited it and saw an amazing building, a great temple with huge stone pillars surmounted by stone sculptures of horses and other animals of gigantic size. It is surrounded by a great empty space enclosed by a strong stone wall upon which human figures are carved with great skill and delicacy. The people who live nearby say they are the images of prophets. The temple stands in front of a mountain, and the winds that blow night and day make a noise like thunder.

The Muslims say that Solomon imprisoned the wind here, and that he breakfasted in Ba'lbakk in the land of Syria and dined in this mosque, breaking his journey at the city of Palmyra, in the desert between Iraq and Damascus and Homs in the land of Syria. It is about a six-days journey from Damascus. It is beautifully built of stone, as is the amphitheatre. It is now inhabited by Arabs of the tribe of Qahtān.

25. *Iram of the Columns*

The great temple known as Jayrūn in the city of Damascus was built by Jayrūn ibn Sa'd of the tribe of 'Ād, who supplied the marble columns which support it. This monument is identical to the Iram of the Columns mentioned in the Qur'ān.

A different story is told on the authority of Ka'b al-Ahbar. When he came to the court of Mu'āwiya ibn Abī Sufyān, Mu'āwiya asked him about Iram. Ka'b described a wonderful building covered with gold and silver and cemented with saffron and musk. He said that an Arab searching for his two lost camels would rediscover Iram, and he described the man. Then, turning to the assembly, he cried out: 'There's the man I just told you about!'

And indeed, this Arab had found Iram while looking for his lost camels. So Mu'āwiya rewarded Ka'b's truthfulness and reliability. If the story related on Ka'b's authority were true, it would be a good thing; unfortunately it is suspect, both for the chain of transmission and for other reasons. It must be considered the invention of the professional storytellers.

The site of Iram of the Columns, and indeed its very existence, has given rise to much discussion. None of the experts in tradition at the court of Mu'āwiya, men who knew most about the history of the Arabs and other ancient peoples, accepted the legend of Iram, with the exception of 'Ubayd ibn Sharya, who gave Mu'āwiya much information on the battles and events of the past. The work of this 'Ubayd is available to the public and well known.

Many learned men believe stories of this sort to be apocryphal: lies invented by the storytellers to gain favour with kings. It is these men who gave their contemporaries the idea of preserving these tales and repeating them in their turn.

Among these collections are works which have come

down to us in translations from Persian, Indian or Greek originals. We have already mentioned the way they were composed. One such book is entitled *Hazar Efsaneh*, 'The Thousand Tales', for that is what *efsaneh* means in Persian. This book is known to the public as *The Thousand and One Nights*. It is the story of a king, his vizier, the vizier's daughter and her slave, Shirazad and Dinazad. A similar book is called *Farzi u Simas*, which includes information on the kings and viziers of India. Another is the *Book of Sindbad*, and there are other compilations of the same kind.

26. *The wine-cups of Alexander*

There is a fishery in the sea around the Pharos of Alexandria in which are found precious stones from which they make the stones of rings. They are like the varieties of stones called *karkand*, *adhrak* and *asab-adhjusham*. It is said they are fragments of Alexander's drinking vessels. When he died, his mother broke them and threw the pieces into the sea at this place. Others say that Alexander collected these stones and threw them into the sea so that there would always be people in the vicinity of the Pharos, for it is the nature of precious stones always to be sought, whether on land or sea, and the place where they are found is always full of people. The stone most commonly found around the Pharos is jasper.

I have seen many jewellers and men who cut the stones called 'occidental' working on jasper to make the stones of rings and other things, especially the stone known as *bāqalamūn*, which is iridescent, shining with the colours red, green and yellow. The iridescence comes from the colour and clarity of the stone, as well as the angle from which it is seen.

The iridescence of the *bāqalamūn* is like that of the plumage of the peacock – I mean the male not the female bird – whose tail and wings are iridescent. I saw these in India. They displayed colours the sight could not identify or number, colours unlike any others, resulting from the mix of colours in their plumage. This results from the size of their bodies and the length of their feathers, because the peacock in India is wonderfully beautiful, while those that are brought to the lands of Islam and lay eggs produce small chicks with dull plumage which does not dazzle the eyes. They only remotely resemble the Indian bird. This is true only of the male bird.

The same is the case with the orange and round citron. They were brought from India after the year 300/912 and transplanted, first to Oman, then to Basra, Iraq and Syria, becoming common in Tarsus and other cities of the Syrian frontier as well as in Antioch, the Syrian coast, Palestine and Egypt, all places where they were previously unknown. They lost the penetrating sweet smell and beautiful colour they had in India because they lacked the air, soil and water of their native land.

27. *The pyramids*

The temples of Egypt are very curious structures, like the one standing at Arsinoe in Upper Egypt, that of Ikhmīm, which is one of the most famous in the country, or that of Samannūd, and others as well.

Then there are the pyramids, which are very high and built in a very remarkable way. Their sides are covered with all kinds of inscriptions, written in the scripts of ancient nations and of kingdoms which no longer exist. No one can read this writing or knows what was intended by it.

Those who have tried to work out the dimensions of the pyramids estimate their height at 400 cubits or even more. As the pyramid rises, it tapers. The width at the base is roughly equal to the height. As we have already said, these buildings bear inscriptions, relating to the sciences, to the properties of things, to magic and to the secrets of nature. They say that one of the inscriptions reads as follows:

'We built them. Let he who wishes to equal us in dominion and attain a fame and power as great as ours destroy these buildings and obliterate their every trace: it is easier to destroy than to create and to scatter than to heap up.'

It is said that one of the Muslim kings began to demolish one of these pyramids, but that all the revenues of Egypt and other lands would not have sufficed to pay for tearing down the blocks of stone and marble of which it was built.

28. The hippopotamus

When the hippopotamus, which lives in the Nile, gets out of the water and heads for some place on dry land, the inhabitants of Egypt conclude that the flood will reach that very point, neither exceeding it nor falling short. It never fails, for their conclusions are derived from long and constant experience.

The hippopotamus, when he leaves the water, is very harmful to the interests of the landowners and to the harvests, for he devours the crops. He comes out of the water at night and heads at once for the farthest point that he intends to reach. Then he returns to the river, grazing on the crops he had previously inspected, as if he had planned in advance exactly what he would eat. After having grazed, he returns to the Nile and drinks; then he leaves his droppings in various places and these give rise to a secondary growth of vegetation.

When his depredations are extensive and the estates are harmed, the landowners scatter several measures of lupin seeds around the place where he emerges. The creature eats them and goes back to the river, but the lupins expand in his belly, which swells and eventually bursts, and he dies. His body floats on the surface of the water and is hauled to shore. One almost never finds crocodiles in the areas inhabited by hippopotamuses. They resemble a horse, but the hooves and tail are different, and forehead is broader.

29. *Electric catfish*

The Nile and the land of Egypt are inhabited by some very strange animals and fish. Among the latter is the fish called *ra''āda*, which is about a cubit long. When one is caught in the net, the fisherman feels his hands and arms shaking and knows that it is there; then he quickly takes it and throws it out of the net. The quivering can be felt even if the creature is touched only with the end of a wooden pole or reed. Galen mentions the electric fish and says that it can be used to provide instant relief from the pain of a severe migraine by being applied live to the head of the sufferer.

30. *The Night of the Bath*

The Night of the Bath is one of the major festivals of Egypt. It falls on the night of the 9th to 10th of the Coptic month of Tubeh, (corresponding to the 6th to 7th of January), and no one sleeps. I was present at the Night of the Bath in the year 330/941, during the period when the Ikhshīd ruler Muhammad ibn Tughj was living in his palace called 'The Chosen One' on the island that separates the two branches of the Nile. He ordered one side of the island and the river bank at Fustāt illuminated with a thousand candles, in addition to the candles and torches lit by the people of the city, Muslim and Christian, to the number of hundreds of thousands, some in boats on the river, others in the houses along the river banks, others on the shore. Everyone took part in the celebration and displayed all the food, drink, fine clothing and vessels of silver and gold that they could, feasting to the sound of musical instruments. It is the most beautiful night in Egypt, the most animated and joyful. The gates of the quarters of the city are unlocked, and everyone bathes in the Nile, for they believe that it will preserve them from all disease and maladies.

31. The secrets of Egyptian temples

At Ikhmīm in Upper Egypt, more than one person has told me that Abū al-Fayd Dhū al-Nūn al-Misrī al-Ikhmīmī, the ascetic, a wise man who founded his own sect and had a personal creed which he followed, was one of those who could explain the secret of these temples, having often visited them and examined a number of the sculptures and inscriptions that they contain [Dhū al-Nūn al-Misrī, 796–861, was a very early Sufi master, ascetic and Gnostic, who also wrote on alchemy and related subjects]. He said:

'In one of these temples, I found an inscription which I have deciphered. It read:

"Beware of freed slaves, young people with no experience, an army made up of slaves, and Copts turned Arab."

'In another temple I read the following inscription:

"Fate is sealed and Destiny laughs."'

He claimed to have seen elsewhere another inscription

written by the same hand as the first and said, after having studied it, that it read:

'Man is ruled by the stars and does not know it. He who commands the stars does what he wishes.'

The people who built these temples were obsessed with astrology and explored the secrets of nature. In particular, they had learned from the study of astrology that a catastrophe threatened the earth, but they could not decide whether fire would destroy the world, or a flood swallow it or, again, whether its inhabitants would perish by the sword. Fearing that learning would be annihilated with mankind, they built these temples and there preserved their knowledge in the form of figures, statues and inscriptions. They built in both stone and earth, keeping the two types of construction separate.

'If the catastrophe foretold', they said, 'is fire, the buildings made of clay will harden like pottery and thus our sciences will be preserved. If, on the other hand, it is a flood, the water will carry away anything built of clay, but the stone will survive. In the case of destruction by the sword, stone and clay buildings will survive.'

According to what is said – but God knows best – these temples date from before the Flood. Others consider them to have been constructed afterwards.

As regards the catastrophe which the Egyptians awaited without knowing for certain whether it would be fire, water or the sword, it is said that it was in fact the sword: a foreign nation and their king invaded Egypt and slaughtered all its inhabitants. Some think it was a lethal epidemic which spread throughout the country. In support of this theory, people point out the burial mounds of the Tinnis district, known as Abū al-Kūm, where the great heaps of corpses of young and old, male and female, are piled up like a mountain of bones. There are also to be found in numerous places in both Upper and Lower Egypt bodies piled upon each other in the depths of caves, tunnels in the rock and catacombs; but no one knows to what race they belong, for neither the Christians nor the Jews recognize them as their ancestors. The Muslims do not know who they are, and history tells us nothing of them. These bodies are clothed and the jewels which once adorned them are often to be found on the neighbouring hills and mountains.

32. Excavations

I have questioned the most learned Copts of Upper Egypt and other provinces on the meaning of the word 'pharaoh', but no one has been able to tell me anything about it, for this name does not exist in their language. Perhaps originally it was the general title of all their kings and then the language changed, just as Pahlavi, the language of ancient Iran, has become Persian, classical Greek has evolved into modern Byzantine, and Himyaritic and many other tongues have changed. You will find in our previous works strange tales of the treasures and monuments of Egypt and the wealth which both its kings and other nations who ruled this land buried in the earth and which are sought even today.

Among the strange anecdotes on this subject is one told by Yaḥyā ibn Bukayr. While 'Abd al-'Azīz ibn Marwān [governor of Egypt, 685–705] was governing Egypt in the name of his brother 'Abd al-Malik, he was visited by a man who wished to give him some information. 'Abd al-'Azīz asked him what it was about, and the man said, 'Under such and such a dome there is a great treasure.' 'Abd al-'Azīz said, 'What evidence do you have of that?'

'A pavement of different-coloured marbles will appear to us not very far down. Digging farther, we have to remove a door made of bronze, above which is a golden column. On top of the column there is a golden cock; his eyes are two rubies worth more than the revenues of the entire world. His wings are encrusted with rubies and emeralds, and his claws grip plates of gold on top of the column.'

'Abd al-'Azīz immediately commanded him to be given several thousand dinars to pay the wages of the labourers hired for the excavations and all the other necessary work.

There was a large *tell* at the site and the men opened a vast trench in the earth, in which the marble slabs which the man had mentioned were brought to light, thus sharpening the greed of 'Abd al-'Azīz, who immediately made over to him new sums of money and increased the number of workmen.

As they went on digging, they uncovered the head of the cock. His appearance was heralded by a light, swift and intense as lightning, which flashed, shining and brilliant from his ruby eyes. Then the wings and then the claws of the cock appeared. Next, they found, all about the column, a colonnade made of different kinds of stone and marble. It was composed of arches and, above the arched doors, niches with statues and figures of people in bronze and gold. Then came sarcophagi of stone whose lids were battened down and enclosed in nets, locked with rods of gold.

'Abd al-'Azīz ibn Marwān came on horseback to visit the scene of the excavations and look at the discoveries. One of those present, less patient, set foot on the steps of a staircase cast in bronze which led down to the finds. When he set foot on the fourth step, two enormous swords sprang out to the left and right of the staircase, meeting at the point where the man stood and slicing him to pieces. His body rolled to the bottom of the staircase. When a part of the corpse hit a certain step, the column shook, the cock gave a strange whistling cry, which was heard at a great distance, and flapped its wings. Terrifying sounds caused by a variety of devices and instruments were heard from beneath him. As soon as an object fell on the steps or only touched them, all who were present slid to the bottom of the excavation. The labourers engaged in digging and moving the earth, those who were supervising and organizing the work and those overseeing the workmen – some two thousand in all – perished to a man.

'Abd al-'Azīz was seized with terror and cried, 'Here are ruins of the most marvellous kind to which all access is forbidden! We seek refuge in God from the evil therein!'

Then he ordered that earth from the excavations should be flung onto the bodies of the victims and that the place should be their tomb.

Some people, interested in excavations and such discoveries, and very eager to dig mounds in order to hunt for the treasures and precious things which the kings and people of Egypt had long ago hidden in the bosom of the earth, found in a book written in ancient characters a description of a place, only a few cubits from the pyramids mentioned above, which promised them a rich treasure. They told the ruler, the Ikhshīd Muhammad ibn Tughj, who gave them permission to excavate and to use all means necessary to reach the aim of their search.

They opened a deep trench and eventually came to vaults, catacombs and hollowed blocks of stone cut into the rock. Inside stood statues. They were coated with a varnish designed to prevent them rotting or wearing away. The figures were of all different kinds: old men, youths, women and children. Their eyes were made of precious stones, such as rubies, emeralds, turquoise and topaz, and some of them had faces made of silver or gold.

After having broken open several of these statues, it became clear that they housed fragments of bone and bodies crumbling into dust. Beside each one was a kind of jar like an amphora of emerald or marble containing the same varnish as had been used upon the corpses lying in their wooden coffers. The jars containing the remains of this substance, which was made of many ingredients, mixed and pounded, had no odour, but when it was tested in a fire it gave off an agreeable aroma different from any other perfume.

Each of the wooden chests had precisely the shape of the body it enclosed, and they varied according to the rank, age and appearance of the dead. In front of each chest was a statue in white or green marble, which was apparently one of the idols that the Egyptians worshipped. Each of these statues bore a different inscription, which no one, of any religion, could decipher. Several learned men maintained that this script disappeared in Egypt 4000 years ago. All of which at least proves that the inhabitants of the country in antiquity were neither Jews nor Christians.

The excavations took place in the year 328/939 and led to no discoveries beyond these figures. From the ancient masters of Egypt up until Ahmad ibn Tūlūn [ruler of Egypt, 878–84] and indeed the present year, 332/944, strange circumstances have led to a series of discoveries of buried objects: money, jewels, treasures and hoards, hidden in tombs. We have already discussed them in our preceding works and in our writings already mentioned.

33. *Upper Egypt and the Oases*

The emerald mine called al-Khirba is seven days' march from any habitation. The nearest towns are Quft, Qūs and various other places in Upper Egypt. Qūs is on the

Nile, while Qufṭ is two miles from the river. The origins of these two towns and their history under the ancient Egyptians are the subject of wondrous tales, but Qufṭ is now threatened with ruin, while Qūs is flourishing and densely populated.

The Beja nomads control al-Allaqi, where the gold mine is located. Al-Allaqi is fifteen stages [days' travel] from the Nile. The inhabitants drink rainwater, although there is a spring in the centre of the town. The nearest town is Aswan, which supplies them with food. The Nubians come with their caravans laden with merchandise to Aswan, whose population is intermixed with Nubians.

The Country of the Oases extends across Egypt, Alexandria, Upper Egypt, the Maghrib and that part of Abyssinia inhabited by Nubians and other peoples. In the present year, 332/943, the Lord of the Oases is called 'Abd al-Malik ibn Marwān. He is of the tribe of the Lawāta [a major Berber tribe], but Marwanid in sympathy. He has at his orders several thousand cavalry, mounted on dromedaries. His lands are roughly six days' march from Abyssinia and about the same from the centres of population that we have just mentioned.

This country, which produces many specialities and has numerous remarkable characteristics, is self-sufficient and independent. Dates, raisins and grapes are brought from this country.

I saw the agent of Lord of the Oases at the court of the Ikhshīd ruler Muhammad ibn Tughj [882–946, governor of Egypt under the 'Abbasids], I questioned him on everything I wanted to know as regards the peculiarities of his native land, for this is the method which I have always used with all the people whose countries I have not been able to visit in person. He told me about the alum, and different kinds of vitriol and other products exported from their land, as well as the bitter springs and other waters with different tastes.

34. The Nubians

The Nubians are divided into two peoples, depending upon whether they have settled on the east or the west bank of the Nile. Their country is contiguous to the territories of the Copts in Upper Egypt, the city of Aswan and other places. They increased their territory by going upstream almost to the upper reaches of the Nile. There they built the capital of their kingdom, a large town called Dongola.

The second branch of the Nubians, called the 'Alwa, also built a city for their king, which they named Soba [near present-day Khartoum].

When I had reached this point in my book at Fustāt in the month of Rabī' II 332/ December 943, I was told that the king of the Nubians living in Dongola was named Kubra ibn Surūr and that he was descended from a long line of kings. He ruled the Muqurra and the 'Alwa. The part of his territory which touches the Aswan region is called Marīs and has lent its name to the wind called *marīsī*. The district of Dongola thus borders the Egyptian districts of Upper Egypt and the town of Aswan.

35. *The sources of the Nile*

The sources of the Nile are in the Mountains of the Moon, which lies 7½ degrees south of the equator, equivalent to 141⅔ farsakhs or 425 miles. Ten streams of water issue forth from these sources, five falling into one lake, five into another. These lakes are situated south of the equator. Three rivers run out of each of these two lakes, and then join together in a single lake situated in the first clime. From this lake the Nile descends into Egypt. It passes through the land of the Blacks, then flows past 'Alwa, capital of the kingdom of Nubia, then through Dongola, also in Nubia. It then leaves the first clime and enters the second at Aswan, a city in Upper Egypt and the first Muslim city beyond the Nubian frontier. After having passed through Upper Egypt it reaches Fustāt and then flows through a number of mouths into the Mediterranean, in the third clime. From the equator to the city of Alexandria on the coast where one of its branches debouches into the sea is a distance of 30°, equivalent to 1820 miles or 606⅔ farsakhs. From the source of the Nile in the Mountains of the Moon to the place where it falls into the Mediterranean is a distance of 748⅔ farsakhs, equivalent to 2245 miles. Some authorities claim that the distance from its origin to its mouth is 1130 farsakhs and a bit.

There are many villages of the Zanj in the vicinity of the Mountains of the Moon. After having passed through them one arrives at the land of Sofala, also in the territory of the Zanj, and the island of Qanbalū, whose inhabitants are Muslim, then to the lands of Berbera and Hafūnī. In our previous works we have explained why these mountains are called the Mountains of the Moon, the remarkable influences the phases of the moon have on them and the opinions of the philosophers, as well as the Manicheans and others on this point.

36. *The Red Sea*

All of the Abyssinian coast of the Red Sea west of Yemen, from Jiddah to the Hijāz, is barren and wretched, producing no trade goods, except tortoise-shell and panther skins. The same is true of the opposite shore, the land of al-Shihr and al-Ahqāf from the coast of Hadramaut to Aden. The whole of this coast is without resources, and its one export today is the incense called *kundur* [frankincense].

This sea, which ends at Qulzum [the ancient port of Clysma, near Suez], is to the right of the Indian Ocean, although in fact their waters form part of the same whole. The Red Sea is the most dangerous of the seas and gulfs that make up the Abyssinian Sea; none has more reefs, and nowhere is one more prone to be seasick. No sea is more sterile and less productive, both as regards its shores and the depths of the sea itself than the Red Sea.

During the sailing season, ships voyage night and day in the rest of the Sea of Abyssinia. In the Red Sea, on the other hand, ships sail only by day. When night falls they drop anchor in known anchorages (just as caravans stop for the night at known campsites) because of its reefs, its darkness and the fear it inspires. Far from sharing in the riches of the Indian Ocean, this sea is completely unendowed.

37. Socotra

In this sea which washes the land of Aden is an island called Socotra, which has lent its name to the Socotran aloe, for this is the only place where it is found and the only place from which it is exported.

Aristotle, the son of Nicomachus, wrote to Alexander, son of Philip, when he set out for India, to tell him about this island and advised him to send a party of Greeks there to settle and exploit the aloes, which are much used as purgatives and other things. So Alexander sent a certain number of Greeks to this island, for the most part natives of Stagira, the hometown of Aristotle, in ships with their families via the Red Sea.

They overcame the Indians who had previously settled on that island and gained control. The Indians had a huge idol which they worshipped, and in a story too long to relate, it was carried off. The Greek population of the island increased and multiplied.

Alexander died, the Messiah came and the inhabitants adopted Christianity, which they still profess today. There is no other place in the world – but God knows best – where the Greek population has preserved its racial purity, without ever intermarrying with the Byzantines, or any other people.

Socotra is at present one of the provisioning points for the Indian pirate ships that harry the Muslim vessels bound for China, India and other places, just as the Byzantine galleys chase the Muslim ships in the Mediterranean along the coasts of Syria and Egypt.

The type of aloes known as Socotran aloes and other medicinal plants are exported from Socotra. A number of details about this island and the medicinal plants and drugs produced there are to be found in our earlier works.

38. *The Zanj*

To return to the Zanj [East Africa and its inhabitants] and their kings: the name given to the kings of that country is *waflimi*, which means 'son of the Great Lord', because it is He who has chosen the king to govern and administer justice. As soon as the king begins to exercise his power in a tyrannical manner, departing from the true way, they kill him and his descendants are forbidden to succeed to the throne, for by behaving in this way he ceases to be the 'son of the Lord', who is the King of Heaven and Earth. They give the Creator the name *Mkulunjulu*, which means 'Great Lord'.

The Zanj express themselves eloquently in their own language and have orators in their own tongue. Often a holy ascetic of the country will gather a numerous crowd about him and exhort his listeners to draw close to God and submit themselves to His will. He warns them of the terrible penalties for disobedience and reminds them of the example of their kings of old and their ancestors. These people have no written religious code of law to which they can refer, but follow the decrees and rulings of their kings by which they are governed.

The Zanj eat bananas, which are common there as they are in India, but the staple food of the Zanj is sorghum and a plant called *kalādī*, which is pulled from the ground like truffles, and the root of the *rāsin*, which is to be found in great quantities in Aden and in those areas of Yemen near that town. *Kalādī* resembles taro, which is found in Egypt and Syria. They also eat honey and meat.

Anyone among them who particularly likes something, be it animal, vegetable or mineral, worships it.

Their islands in the sea are innumerable. The coconut palm grows in them and provides one of the foods eaten by all the Zanj peoples. One of these islands, called Qanbalū [either Zanzibar or Pemba], a day or two distant from the coast, has a Muslim population with inherited kingship.

39. *The Indian Ocean*

The size of the Indian Ocean, which is also called the Sea of Abyssinia, has been calculated. Its length from west to east, from the farthest point of Abyssinia to the farthest point of India and China, is 8000 miles, while its width is 2700 miles, although another source gives 1900. Some authorities give a smaller width, others a greater. The figures we have given for its length and breadth differ in other sources, but we will pass over these estimates because they are not based on convincing figures supplied by professionals.

This sea contains a gulf which extends to the land of Abyssinia, passing the district of Berbera in the land of the Zanj and the Abyssinians. It is called the Berbera Gulf and is 500 miles long and its two shores are 100 miles apart. This Berbera should not be confused with the country of the Berbers in Ifrīqīya in North Africa, which is completely different, and has nothing in common with this Berbera except its name. Sailors from Oman cross this gulf to reach the island of Qanbalū, which lies in the Sea of Zanj. This island is inhabited by a mixed population of Muslims and pagan Zanj.

The Omani sailors mentioned above maintain that the Berbera Gulf, which they call the 'Sea of Berbera and the land of Hafūnī', is larger than we have said. They say its waves are like great mountains. They form troughs like deep valleys, but never break and are never covered with the foam one sees when waves break in

the middle of the sea. They say these waves are crazy.
The Omani sailors who voyage in this sea are from the
tribe of Azd. When they are in the middle of the
sea and find themselves among the waves we have
mentioned, rising and falling, they sing these verses as
they manoeuvre:

> Berbera and Hafūnī
> And your crazy waves!
> Berbera and Hafūnī
> Its waves are as you see!

Their destination in the Sea of Zanj is the island of
Qanbalū, as we have said, and the lands of Sofala and
Wāqwāq [probably Madagascar], which are on the
farthest reaches of the land of Zanj and the lower
reaches of this sea. The people of Sīrāf [a major port
on the Persian Gulf in the tenth century] sail this sea
and so did I, voyaging from the city of Suhār, capital
of the land of Oman, in the company of ships' captains
from Sīrāf. Among them were mariners such as
Muhammad ibn al-Zaydabūd and Jawhar ibn Ahmad,
known as Ibn Sīra, who perished in this sea along with
his entire ship's company.

My last crossing from the island of Qanbalū to
Oman was in 304/916–17. I was on a ship belonging to
Ahmad and 'Abd al-Samad, both brothers of 'Abd
al-Rahīm ibn Ja'far al-Sīrāfī of Mīkān, a quarter of
Sīrāf. They went down with their ship in this sea, along
with everyone who was with them, I mean Ahmad and
'Abd al-Samad, the two sons of Ja'far. At the time of

my last voyage, the emir of Oman was Ahmad ibn Hilāl, son of the sister of al-Qaytāl.

I have sailed many seas, the Sea of China, the Mediterranean, the Sea of the Khazars, the Red Sea and the Sea of Yemen, and I have been afflicted with terrors past numbering, but I have never seen any sea more terrifying than the Sea of Zanj I have just described.

40. Brahman the Great

Scholars of discernment and judgement, who have pondered the nature and origin of the world, have stated that the Indians in ancient times were particularly endowed with righteousness and wisdom. When societies began to be formed and political divisions came into being, the Indians sought to unify the kingdom and to take control of power, so that they might become the rulers. Their leaders said, 'We were the people of the beginning; to us belong the limit and the ultimate object; in us is contained the beginning and the end. It was from among us that the father of mankind originated and went out to populate the earth. We shall not tolerate rebels or resistance and shall overpower and annihilate anyone who impedes us, unless he once again becomes obedient.'

Having taken this decision, they chose a king, Brahman the Great, who was the mightiest of their kings and the foremost of their lawgivers. During his reign, wisdom flourished and learned men were favoured. They extracted iron from the mines, and swords, daggers and a variety of the implements of war were manufactured. Brahman constructed temples and embellished them with shining precious stones, depicting the spheres, the twelve signs of the zodiac and the stars. He not only depicted the nature of the universe, but explained with the help of pictures how the celestial bodies act upon this world and produce living things, rational and otherwise. Brahman also explained the workings of the prime mover, namely the sun. He set down the evidence for all this in his book, in such a way that it could be understood by the common people, while the notion of a superior being was at the same time implanted in the minds of the educated classes, a 'prime mover' which gives rise to everything in existence and penetrates everything with its beneficence.

The Indians submitted to this king, and their country flourished as he showed them ways to improve their lives. During his reign, men of wisdom collaborated and produced the treatise entitled *al-Sindhind* [*Siddhānta*], which means 'the age of ages'. From this work were derived others, such as *al-Arjabhad* [*Āryabhatīya*] and *al-Majisti* [*Almagest*]. From *al-Arjabhad* was derived *al-Arkand* [*Khandakhādyaka*], and *al-Majistī*, the book of Ptolemy, from which they calculated astronomical tables. Then they invented the nine numerals which comprise the Indian number system.

Brahman was the first to define the apogee of the sun. He stated that the sun remains in each sign of the zodiac for 3000 years and traverses the whole sphere of the heavens in 36,000 years. According to the

Brahmans the apogee of the sun in our own time, which is the year 332/943, lies in the sign of Gemini; when it passes into the southern signs of the zodiac, the face of the earth will change accordingly, the inhabited regions becoming barren and the barren regions becoming inhabited. North will become south and south become north.

Brahman deposited calculations in the House of Gold pertaining to the date of the appearance of the Buddha and the chronology which the Indians use for calculating his subsequent appearances in the land of India, to the exclusion of other countries. The Indians have elaborate theories about this, which we shall not mention here, for ours is a book on history, not a book of theory and opinion. In any case, we have given a survey of the subject in our *Intermediate History*.

41. Multān

The ruler of Multān is a descendant of Sāma ibn Lu'ayy ibn Ghālib, who was commander of a powerful army. Multān is an important frontier region for the Muslims with an official census of 120,000 villages and hamlets. It has, as we have already said, an idol known as Multān, and people come from the farthest reaches of Sind and India to bring offerings of money and of precious stones, aloes-wood and all kinds of scents; thousands of people make this pilgrimage. The king of Multān derives the largest portion of his revenues from the valuable aromatic woods that are brought to this idol, especially the pure aloe-wood of Cambodia, a *mann* [about 13 pounds] of which is worth 200 dinars, and which takes the imprint of a seal-like wax – not to mention the other marvels that are offered. Every time the infidel kings march against Multān and the Muslims find themselves in no condition to resist, they threaten to break the idol or mutilate it, which is enough to convince their enemies to retreat. When I arrived in that city some time after the year 300/912–13, the ruling prince was called Abū al-Lahhāb al-Munabbih ibn Asad al-Qurashī al-Sāmiyy.

42. War elephants

An agile, well-trained, brave elephant, ridden by a good mahout, its trunk armed with the kind of sabre known as a *qartal* and covered with chain mail, while the rest of its body is protected by sheets of bark and iron, surrounded by 500 men to defend it and protect it to the rear, can fight against 6000 men on horseback. There is not one that with an escort of 500 could not attack at least 5000, penetrating their ranks and then drawing back to harass them from every direction, just as a horseman might. This is the usual way they deploy elephants in all their wars.

The king of Mansūra has eighty war elephants. It is the custom that each elephant should be surrounded by 500 foot soldiers and thus he can fight thousands of cavalry, as we have already explained. I saw two elephants in this ruler's possession of the most enormous size, famous among all the kings of Sind and India for their strength, courage and daring in combat. One was called Manfarqalas and the other Haydara. All kinds of remarkable deeds and outstanding characteristics are attributed to Manfarqalas. They are famous in those lands and in the neighbouring countries. Once, when one of his mahouts died, he remained for days without eating or drinking, showing his grief and sorrow like a man bereaved, tears flowing ceaselessly from his eyes.

Another time, Manfarqalas, followed by Haydara and the other eighty elephants, left his stable. On passing through a narrow street in Mansūra, he found himself face to face with a woman who was completely taken aback by the sight. Struck with terror, the unfortunate woman panicked and fell backwards in the middle of the street, revealing her private parts. When Manfarqalas saw that, he stopped and stood sideways across the street, presenting his right flank to the other elephants who were following him, to prevent them from advancing. Then, waving his trunk as if signing to the woman to get up, he pulled down her dress with his trunk, thus covering the parts of her body that had been revealed. It was only after she had got up, come to her senses and got out of the road that he continued on his way, followed by his companions.

43. *The Balharā of Mānkīr*

The reign of Balhīt lasted 80 years, or, according to other versions, 130 years. His successor, Kūrush, abandoned the doctrines of his predecessors and introduced to India religious innovations more suited to the times and interests of his contemporaries. During his reign lived Sindbad, the author of *The Book of the Seven Viziers, the Young Slave and the Wife of the Ring*, that is, the book known as the *Book of Sindbad*. It was in the library of this king that a great work on pathology and therapeutics was composed, with illustrations and drawings of various plants. He died after a reign of 120 years.

At his death, discord broke out among the Indians. They divided into a number of nations and tribes, each ruled by its own chief. This is how kings came to reign in Sind, Kanauj and Kashmīr. Mānkīr [Malkhed, south of Gulbarga in Andhra Pradesh], the leading city of India, was taken by a king named Balharā [Vallabha Raja, 'beloved king']; this was the name of the first ruler of this kingdom, but it became the dynastic title of his successors on the throne of Mānkīr and has remained so until our days, 332/943.

The most powerful king now reigning in India is the Balharā, king of the city of Mānkīr. Most of the kings of India turn their faces towards him when praying and bow before his ambassadors when they arrive at their courts. The territories of the Balharā are surrounded by many principalities. Some of these kings live in mountainous regions, far from the sea; among them are the Raja of Kashmīr and the king of Thakka. Other states are both continental and maritime. The capital of the Balharā is 80 Sindī farsakhs from the sea [the Sindī farsakh is equivalent to 8 miles]. His armies and elephants are innumerable, but almost all his troops are infantry, because his capital is in the mountains.

44. *The tide at Cambāya*

This is something I saw in the land of India, in the region of Cambāya, known for its noisy sandals of the sort known as 'Cambāyan sandals', which are made there in the neighbouring towns, such as Sandān and Sufāra. I arrived at Cambāya in the year 303/915–16, when a Brahmin called Bānīyā was governing in the name of Balharā, the lord of Mānkīr. This Bānīyā was very interested in having debates with Muslims and the followers of other faiths who arrived in his country.

The city of Cambāya stands on a deep bay, a gulf wider than the Nile, the Tigris or the Euphrates, whose shores are covered with cities, estates, cultivated fields, gardens and coconut plantations. Between these gardens and the water are to be seen peacocks, parrots and other kinds of bird that are found in India. It is a little less than two days' journey from the city to the sea which forms this inlet. Nevertheless, the tidal bore makes itself felt with such force that the sand at the bottom can be clearly seen. I saw a dog lying on this sand, which the water had left dry and which resembled a desert. Suddenly the tide rushed in, as fast as horses during a race. The dog, scenting danger, began to run as fast as it could to escape the water and reach the land above the tide line, but the swiftly moving waves engulfed it as it ran and drowned it.

45. The rhinoceros

In this country lives the animal known as the dappled *bishān*, called *karkaddan* by the common people. It has a single horn on its forehead and is smaller than an elephant, but larger than a water buffalo; it is blackish in colour and chews the cud, as do oxen and other ruminants. The elephant flees from it and no creature – but God knows best – is stronger than it. That is because most of its bones are fused together, so that its legs cannot bend and it can neither kneel nor lie down to sleep, and so it sleeps leaning against trees in the jungle.

The Indians eat its flesh, and so do the Muslims who live in their countries, because it is of the same species as the cow and water buffalo, the latter being very numerous in India and Sind. The rhinoceros is found in most of the wooded areas of India, but nowhere in such great quantity as within the confines of the kingdom of Dahram, where its horn is of a special beauty and lustre. The horn of the rhinoceros is white with a black figure in the centre, which represents the form of a man or a peacock, showing the outline and the shape of the tail, or a fish, or the rhinoceros itself, or some other creature of these regions.

They saw up these horns and make them into belts using thongs, just as is done with gold and silver ornaments. The kings and their courtiers in China wear them, rivalling each other in the amount they will pay for them, spending as much as 2000 and even 4000 dinars for one. The clasps are of gold, and the whole is of an extraordinary beauty and strength. Often, different sorts of precious stones are attached to them with golden nails. The figures we have mentioned are usually traced in black on the white part of the horn, but sometimes they are in white on a black ground. Rhinoceros horn does not have these figures we have mentioned in all countries.

Jāhiz [the leading writer of his time, a master of Arabic literary prose and a notable polymath, 776–869] claims that the female carries her offspring for seven years, during which time the young animal pushes his head out of his mother's belly in order to graze and then goes back in. He has mentioned this fact as a remarkable and amusing peculiarity in his *Book of Animals*. Wishing to clear up this point for my own interest, I questioned the inhabitants of Sirāf and Oman who have often been in these countries, as well as the merchants whom I met in India; all were equally surprised at the question. They stated very positively that the rhinoceros gives birth exactly like a cow or a buffalo. I do not know where Jāhiz got his story, whether he copied it from a book or heard it from some informant.

46. Saymūr

In 304/916 I was in the district of Saymūr [present-day Chaul] in India; it is in the province of Lār, which forms part of the kingdom of the Balharā. The reigning prince was named Janj. There were some 10,000 Muslims, both *bayāsira* and natives of Sirāf, Oman, Basra, Baghdād and other cities who had married there and permanently settled. Among them were wealthy merchants, such as Mūsā ibn Ishāq al-Sandabūrī and the *hazma* of the time, Abū Sa'īd Ma'rūf ibn Zakariyā; *hazma* means leader of the Muslim community. In this country the king appoints one of the most distinguished members of the community to this position, and delegates responsibility for its affairs to him. The word *bayāsira*, singular *baysar*, means someone born in India of Muslim parents; this is what they are called.

47. Betel

The betel leaf is found in these countries. It is the size of a small basil leaf. It is chewed with a mixture of lime and areca nut. This habit has spread in our days to the Meccans, as well as other people of the Hijāz and Yemen; it has replaced the chewing of mastic. It can be found in pharmacies and is used against swollen gums and similar ills. Some call it *fawfal*. Areca nuts crushed with betel leaves and lime reinforces the gums, strengthens the teeth and gives the breath an agreeable odour. It counters cold humours, excites the appetite and is an aphrodisiac. It stains the teeth the colour of the ripest pomegranate seeds, provokes gaiety and good humour, strengthens the body and spreads a delicious and delicate scent. The Indians, rich and poor, dislike white teeth and avoid the society of those who do not use the mixture we have described.

48. *The banyan tree*

There is a tree in this country which can be considered one of the marvels of nature and prodigies of the vegetable kingdom. It spreads over the ground with interlaced branches of the most beautiful appearance and richest foliage; it reaches up in the air to the height of the tallest palm trees, then its branches curve down in the opposite direction, forcing themselves into the earth, which they penetrate little by little to a depth equal to the height they had grown above ground, disappearing from view. Then they reappear with new branches, which rise up like the first, descend and open a passage through the earth. The branches that rise up into the air and grow there and those that hide themselves from view under the ground are the same size. If the Indians did not employ men to prune them, and, for religious reasons having to do with the next life, look after these trees, they would cover the country, completely invading it. The trees have a number of other peculiarities that it would take too long to mention here, but which are known to all travellers who have visited these countries and seen them with their own eyes and listened to all they have been told on this subject.

49. Ivory

The kings and civil and military officers in China carry ivory canes. No functionary or notable is allowed to enter the king's presence with an iron object, but only with one of these ivory canes. They therefore search for the straightest elephant tusks, those with the least curve, to make the canes of which we speak. They also burn ivory in their idol temples and use it to perfume their altars, as the Christians use 'Mary's incense' and other aromatics in their churches.

The Chinese do not use elephants and consider it bad luck to acquire them and use them for war. This fear has its origin in a tradition which dates back to one of their most ancient military expeditions.

In India ivory is used a great deal. They employ it for the pommels of the knives called *jarrī*, plural *jarārī*, as well as the hilts of the curved swords called *qartal*, plural *qarātil*.

But the most frequent use of ivory is in the fabrication of chesspieces and backgammon checkers. Many chesspieces are human and animal figures, a span high and wide, or even more. A man is employed to move the pieces from one square to another during the game.

When the Indians play chess or backgammon, they bet lengths of cloth or precious stones. Sometimes a player, having lost all he has, bets one of his body parts. For this purpose a little copper pot filled with a red salve peculiar to the country is placed beside each player on a brazier. The salve heals wounds and staunches the flow of blood. If a player has bet one of his fingers and loses, he cuts it off with the sort of knife we mentioned, and it cuts like fire. Then he plunges his hand into the salve and cauterizes the wound. Then he plays again. If he loses, he cuts off a second finger. Sometimes, if the game goes against him, he cuts off all his fingers, his hand, forearm, elbow and other parts of his body. He cauterizes the wound after each amputation with the salve, which is a wondrous mixture of drugs and ingredients indigenous to India, whose effects are remarkable. What I have just related of their behaviour is well known.

50. Backgammon

It was at this time that backgammon was invented and began to be popular. It is a kind of paradigm of how wealth is acquired, which in this world is not the reward of intelligence or ability, just as luck is not a product of skill. Ardashīr, son of Bābak [founder of the Sasanian dynasty, 224–42], is also credited with the invention and playing of this game, which was inspired by the spectacle of the vicissitudes of fortune and the caprices of destiny. He divided the board into twelve 'houses', according to the number of months, with thirty checkers to represent the days. The two dice represent fate and its effect on men. If luck favours the player, he gets what he wants; if it doesn't, a skilled and prudent man cannot win that which fortune only bestows on whom it likes. It is thus that the good things of this world are apportioned by chance.

51. *The Invention of chess*

Bahbūd was succeeded by Zāmān, who reigned 150 years. The main events of this reign and his wars with the kings of Persia and China have been outlined in our previous works. He was succeeded by Porus, who did battle with Alexander and was killed by him in single combat. He had reigned 140 years.

He was succeeded by Dabshalim, the author of the *Panchatantra*, translated into Arabic by Ibn al-Muqaffa'. Sahl ibn Hārūn composed a work with the title *Tha'la wa 'Afrā'* for the caliph Ma'mūn, which is an imitation, both in plan and the nature of the fables, of *Kalila wa Dimna*, but is superior to it because of the elegance of its style. Dabshalim reigned 110 years, but there is no agreement about this.

He was succeeded by Balhīt. It was at this time that the game of chess was invented, which eclipsed backgammon by demonstrating how intelligence brings success and ignorance failure. The king worked out mathematical models for chess and composed a book on this subject called *Taraq Jankā*, still popular among Indians. He often played chess with the wise men of his court, and it was he who gave the pieces human and animal shapes, assigned them grades and ranks, and made the king the one who rules all the other pieces. He also made this game an allegory of the heavenly bodies, that is to say, of the seven planets and the signs of the zodiac. He consecrated each piece to a star and made it the guardian of the kingdom. When one of their enemies employed a ruse of war against them, they consulted the chessboard to see from which point they would sooner or later be attacked.

52. The kings of India and Sarandīb

In India, a king cannot ascend the throne until he reaches the age of forty. He shows himself to the people only briefly, at specified times and then exclusively to examine the condition of his subjects, for according to their ideas a king would harm his dignity and no longer inspire the same respect if he appeared before the common people all the time. Leaders are chosen for their qualities, with due respect for their position in the political hierarchy.

This is what I saw in the land of Sarandīb [Sri Lanka], one of the islands in the Indian Ocean. When a king dies they place him on a low cart with small wheels, intended for the purpose, in such a way that his hair trails on the ground. A woman with a broom in her hand throws dust on the head of the dead man, crying:

'People! Behold your king of yesterday! He was your master; his slightest whims were obeyed. Now he has become what you see before you! He has left this world and his soul is in the hands of the King of Death, the Living, the Eternal, He who dies not! Therefore do not yield to the illusions of this life!'

She continues exhorting the people in this vein, inspiring them with fear and urging them to detach themselves from worldly pleasures. Then, having taken the body through all the streets of the city, they cut it in four pieces and burn it on a pyre made of sandalwood, camphor and other aromatics. Then they scatter the ashes to the winds.

These are the ceremonies which almost all the Indians perform for their kings and great men, and for which they give reasons connected with their beliefs about the afterlife.

Kingship is confined to a single royal lineage and never passes to another. The same is true of ministers, judges and all the high officials, who are always from the same families.

The Indians forbid the drinking of wine and blame those who do so, not because their religion forbids it, but because they are afraid it will trouble their reason and deprive them of the use of this faculty. If one of their kings is found to have drunk wine, he is thought to deserve to be deposed, for it would be impossible for him to govern the state when his reason is clouded.

They are very fond of singing and music and have a variety of musical instruments, which evoke a whole range of emotions in men, from laughter to tears. Often they have young slave girls drink and dance before them, in order to rouse themselves to a state of joy at the sight of their gaiety.

From *The Meadows of Gold*

53. *Kashmīr*

Another river [the Kabul River] has its source in Kash-mīr, whose king generally bears the title *raja*. Kashmīr is one of the mountain kingdoms of Sind. It is a very large kingdom, with no less than 60,000 or 70,000 towns and villages. It is only accessible on one side, and can be entered only via a single pass. It is enclosed by steep, impassable mountains that no one can climb. Even wild beasts cannot reach their summits; only birds can fly that high. Where the mountains cease there are hidden valleys, forest, jungles and swift, unfordable rivers. What we have said here about the impossibility of crossing the mountains of Kashmīr is well known in Khurāsān and elsewhere, and makes Kashmīr one of the wonders of the world.

54. *Tibet*

Tibet is a kingdom distinct from China. The majority of the population is of Himyarite origin and includes some descendants of the Tubba'[the Himyarite kings, the pre-Islamic rulers of Yemen], as we shall explain further on in this work, when dealing with the kings of Yemen, and as may also be found in the *History of the Tubba'*. Some of the Tibetans are sedentary, while others are nomads. The second group are Turks by origin and innumerable; no other Turkic people can equal them. They are much honoured by all the nomad tribes of their race, because they once held sway over all the rest, and the Turkic peoples believe that one day they will do so again.

Tibet is unique and strange in its climate, water, earth, mountains and plains. Its inhabitants are always happy and laughing; they are never to be seen sad, downcast or depressed. The marvellous varieties of fruit and flowers found in this kingdom cannot be numbered, nor can the richness of its pasturelands and rivers be described. The climate strengthens the nature of the blood of all living things, whether men or beasts, and it is very rare to meet with a sad old man or woman. As a general thing, good humour seems to reign there in middle and advanced age, just as in adolescence and in youth. The innate sweet nature, gaiety and liveliness with which all Tibetans are endowed leads them to cultivate music with great passion and give themselves over to every kind of game and different kinds of dancing.

Even death itself does not inspire relatives with that profound grief which other men must feel when their beloved is snatched away and they lament one who was most dear. Nevertheless, they feel great affection for each other, and the adoption of orphans is very general among them. The animals likewise are endowed with natural goodness.

Tibet borders China on one side and on the other India, Khurāsān and the steppes of the Turks. There are many densely populated, flourishing, well-defended towns.

In ancient times, the kings bore the title of *tubba'* after Tubba', king of Yemen. Then, the erosion of time wore away the language of the Himyarites, putting in its place the tongue of the neighbouring people, and the kings were given the title of *khāqān*.

55. *The Silk Road*

China is watered by rivers as large as the Tigris and the Euphrates, whose sources lie in the country of the Turks, in Tibet and in Sogdiana, between Bukhara and Samarkand, where the mountains of sal ammoniac are located. During the summer, fires can be seen at night rising from these mountains from a distance of 100 farsakhs. During the daytime, only the smoke can be seen, due to the brightness of the sun's rays and the light of day. Sal ammoniac is exported from these mountains. When winter comes, the traveller who wishes to go from Khurāsān to China comes to this district, where there is a valley between the mountains which extends for 40 or 50 miles. At the entrance to the valley, the traveller encounters people who for a high price will carry his baggage on their shoulders. They carry a stick in their hands with which they prod the traveller in the sides for fear that dropping with fatigue he will stop and perish from the torments of this valley. They walk in front of him until they reach the end of the valley, where they find thickets and stagnant water into which everyone throws themself to recover from the torments of the journey and the heat of the sal ammoniac.

The beasts of burden do not follow this route,

because the sal ammoniac catches fire during the summer and makes it impassable. In the winter, the great quantity of snow which falls in these places and the dampness extinguish the burning, so men can cross it, but the animals cannot endure the unbearable heat. The same violent attacks with the stick are inflicted on travellers coming out of China.

The distance from Khurāsān to China along the route we have been describing is around forty days' march across cultivated and desert land, with soft sandy soil. There is another route, accessible to pack animals, which takes around four months, but there the travellers are under the protection of the Turkish tribes. I met a handsome old man in Balkh, known for his discernment and intelligence, who had made the journey to China many times, without ever taking the sea route. I also met many people in Khurāsān who had travelled from Sogdiana to Tibet and China, passing by way of the mountains of sal ammoniac.

56. Pearl fishing in the Gulf

Pearl fishing in the Persian Gulf takes place only between the beginning of April and the end of September. It ceases completely during the other months. In our earlier works, we have named all the places in this sea where there are pearl fisheries, for pearls are found exclusively in the Indian Ocean, in the lands of Khark, Qatar, Oman and Sarandīb, and other points along these shores. We have also discussed the manner in which the pearl forms and the different theories advanced on this subject. Some say it is produced by the rain, while others attribute to it an altogether different origin. We have also explained how a distinction is made between old shells and new, which are known as *al-mahār* and also under the name of *al-balbal*.

The flesh and fat which is inside the oyster shell is a living creature, which at the approach of divers, fears on behalf of its pearl as a mother would fear for her child.

We have also explained how the diving is done. The divers, as we have said, do not eat meat and live exclusively on fish and dates. They have their ear lobes split to allow them to expel air, since their nostrils are plugged with a gadget shaped like an arrowhead and made out of tortoiseshell – that is, the same kind of sea-turtle shell which is used for combs. It may also be made of horn, but not of wood. They put cotton soaked in a little oil in their ears, and when they are at the bottom of the sea they squeeze some out, which gives them a little light. They rub their feet and thighs with a black substance, and this causes the monsters of the deep, by which they fear to be dragged down, to flee far away. When they are at the bottom of the sea, they make sounds like the barking of dogs, and this piercing noise serves as a means of communication among them.

The Sea of Persia begins in the region of Basra, al-Ubulla and Bahrayn [eastern Arabia], just after the Basra watchtowers. Then comes the Sea of Lārwī, which washes the coastal cities of Saymūr, Sopara, Tana, Sandān, Cambāya and other ports of India and

Sind. Then comes the Sea of Harkand, then the Sea of Kalāhbār, which is the sea of Kalāh, and the islands. Then follows the Sea of Kanduranj, then the Sea of Sanf and, finally, the Sea of China, or Sanjī, which is the last of all.

57. The first sea: the Sea of Persia

As we have said, the Sea of Persia [the Persian Gulf] begins at the watchtowers of Basra, in the place called al-Kankalā. These are pilings driven into the seabed which serve as signals for ships. It is 300 farsakhs along the coast of Fars and Bahrayn to Oman. The capital of Oman is Suhār, called Mazūn by the Persians. It is a distance of 50 farsakhs from Suhār to Muscat, a city which has wells where ships' captains can take on fresh water. It is 50 farsakhs again from Muscat to Ra's al-Jumjuma, the end of the Sea of Persia, whose length is 400 farsakhs, according to the estimation of sailors and pilots. Ra's al-Jumjuma is a mountain which extends into Yemen, to al-Shihr and al-Ahqāf. In the form of a sandbar it extends under the sea an unknown distance. In the Mediterranean when a mountain extends like this under the sea it is given the name *sufāla*, like the one that extends under the sea in the direction of Cyprus from the area known as the coast of Seleucia in the land of the Byzantines; it is upon this *sufāla* that so many Byzantine ships have run aground and been destroyed. We use the terms current in each sea among sailors.

58. *The second sea: the Sea of Lārwī*

After passing Ra's al-Jumjuma, ships leave the Sea of Persia and enter the second sea, the Sea of Lārwī [Arabian Sea]. Its depth is unknown and its limits cannot be exactly defined because of the extent of its waters and its immensity. Many mariners maintain that it is difficult to give it an exact geographical description because it has so many ramifications. Ships usually take two or three months to cross it, but only one month when the wind is favourable and navigation safe, although this is the largest and stormiest of all the seas collectively known as the Indian Ocean. It joins the Sea of Zanj and the Zanj coast to the south. There is little ambergris in this sea, for most of it is found on the Zanj coast and in al-Shihr in the land of the Arabs.

59. *Ambergris*

The best ambergris is found in al-Shihr and on the coasts of the islands of Zābaj [Sumatra and the other islands of the Indonesian archipelago]. It is round, pale blue, and sometimes the size of an ostrich egg or smaller. Some pieces are swallowed by whales, of which we have already spoken. When the sea is rough, the whale vomits pieces of ambergris, sometimes the size of a piece of mountain, sometimes of the smaller size we have mentioned. Swallowing the ambergris kills the whale, and its corpse floats on the water. The men of

Zābaj and elsewhere hunt it in little boats and attack it with harpoons attached to cables, cut open its belly and remove the ambergris. The ambergris found in its entrails has a sickening smell; the druggists of Iraq and Persia call it *nadd*. That which is found near its back is much purer; the longer it has been inside its body, the purer it is.

60. *The third sea: the Sea of Harkand*

Between the third sea, which is the Sea of Harkand [the Bay of Bengal] and the Sea of Lārwī there are a great many islands, which serve to separate the two seas. It is commonly said that there are 2000 of these islands [the Laccadives and Maldives]; a more precise figure is 1900. They are all densely populated and are governed by a woman, for since the most remote times the inhabitants of these islands have had the tradition of never allowing themselves to be governed by a man.

Ambergris is found in these islands as well, thrown up on the shore by the sea; the lumps are the size of the largest rocks. More than one ship's captain from Sirāf and Oman, and many merchants who have often sailed to these islands, have told me that ambergris grows in the depths of this sea and is formed like black and white mushrooms, truffles or other plants of the same type. When the sea is rough and violent, it throws rocks and pebbles, as well as pieces of ambergris, up from its depths.

The inhabitants of these islands are all governed by

one power. Their number cannot be counted, nor can the troops of this queen. Each island is a mile from its neighbour, or one, two, or three farsakhs. The islands are all planted with coconut palms, which closely resemble date palms but do not bear dates. Many scholars who have specialized in the growth of animals and the grafting of trees claim that the coconut palm is nothing more than the palm called *muql*, which under the influence of the soil of India, where it was transplanted, was transformed into the coconut palm.

61. Craftsmen and cowries

Nowhere among the islands of this sea can such skilled craftsmen, whether it is a matter of textiles, utensils, or other objects, be found as among the people of Dībajāt [the Maldives and Laccadives]. The queen's treasure consists of cowries, which are shells that contain a type of living creature. When her funds run low, she orders the islanders to cut branches from the coconut palms with all their leaves and to throw them on the surface of the water. The shellfish climb on to them as best they can and they are collected and laid out on the sand along the shore, where the sun burns them up, leaving only the empty shells with which the treasury is replenished.

62. Camphor

These islands are known as the Dībajāt. Their main export is coconut, which they call *ranaj*. The last of these islands is Sarandīb. About 1000 farsakhs from Sarandīb there are yet more inhabited islands called al-Rāmnī [western Sumatra], ruled by kings and rich in gold mines. They are close to the land of Fansūr [Barus in western Sumatra], from which comes the type of camphor known as *fansuri*. In the years in which there are many thunderstorms, lightning flashes, earth tremors, falling meteorites and earthquakes, the camphor is abundant, but it is rare in years in which these phenomena are few.

63. The Nicobar and Andaman Islands

Most of the islands we have just mentioned use the coconut for food. *Baqqam* [Brazil wood], bamboo and gold are exported as well. Elephants are numerous, and some of the islands are inhabited by men who eat human flesh. These islands adjoin others, known as the *Lanjabālūs* [Nicobars], where there live a people with strange faces who go naked. They go out in canoes to meet passing boats with ambergris, coconuts and other things which they exchange for iron and certain types of clothing. They do not sell their goods for silver or gold coins. Nearby are the Andaman Islands, which are inhabited by strange-looking blacks with peppercorn hair and feet more than a span long. They have no ships and eat the corpses of shipwrecked sailors that the sea throws up on their shores, as well as the crews of boats that fall into their hands.

64. Waterspouts

Several ship's captains have told me that in this sea they have often seen small white clouds from which a long white tongue extends, stretching down to join the surface of the sea, which immediately begins to boil and great waterspouts spiral up, engulfing everything that stands in their way, and then fall back as rain with a disagreeable smell and mixed with sea spray.

65. The fourth sea: the Sea of Kalāhbār

The fourth sea is, as we have already said, that of Kalāhbār, in other words the Sea of Kalāh [Kedah on the Malaysian Peninsula]. It is shallow, and such shallow seas are dangerous and hard to navigate. There are many islands, and what the mariners call *surr*, which refers to the place where two gulfs meet. There are some very remarkable islands and mountains which we shall not mention, because our aim is to give the briefest outline and on no account to go into details.

66. *The fifth sea: the Sea of Kanduranj*

The fifth sea, known as the Sea of Kanduranj [Gulf of Siam], also has many shoals and islands, in which camphor and 'water of camphor' are found. The sea is shallow, and it almost never stops raining. Among the islanders, who belong to different races, there are some called Fanjan. They have peppercorn hair and frightening faces. Riding in their boats, they go out to meet ships which sail near their shores and shoot them with a strange type of poisoned arrow. Between the country where this people live and the land of Kalāh, there are mines of white lead and silver-bearing mountains. There are also gold and lead mines, but the two metals are difficult to separate.

67. *The sixth sea: the Sea of Sanf*

The Sea of Sanf [South China Sea] comes next after the Sea of Kanduranj, following the order that we established at the beginning. Here is to be found the kingdom of the Maharaja, the King of the Isles, who commands a boundless realm and innumerable troops. Even in the fastest boat, no one could sail all around the islands that he rules in less than two years. This kingdom produces every sort of spice and aromatic, and no king in the world obtains so much wealth from his country. Exported from his country are aloe-wood, cloves, sandalwood, nutmeg, mace, cardamoms and cubebs, as well as other products that we shall not mention.

68. *The ring of fire*

These islands are on the edge of a sea which is next to the Sea of China, but its outer limits cannot be reached and its extent is quite unknown. In the interior of the islands are many mountains inhabited by people with white faces, split ears, faces like pieces of shields, with hair cut in layers like the bristles on a water bottle. Day and night fire issues from the mountains; by day it is red, at night its colour darkens, the flames reaching the highest point of the heavens because of the height of the mountains and then disappearing in the atmosphere. These eruptions are accompanied by terrible rolls of thunder and often also by a strange and terrible voice announcing the death of their king, or when it is less powerful, the passing of some important person. The local people are able to understand these portents, having learned from long experience and the regularity of the occurrences. These mountains are to be numbered among the great volcanoes of the earth.

69. *The island of music*

Nearby is the island from which the sound of drums, flutes, lutes and every kind of musical instrument whose sound is sweet and agreeable is heard, as well as the rhythmic beating of feet and clapping of hands. By listening carefully, the sounds of each instrument can easily be distinguished. The sailors who cross these seas claim that the Antichrist has taken up his abode there.

The island of Sribuza [Srivijaya] lies within the kingdom of the Maharaja; it is about 400 farsakhs in length and entirely cultivated. He also possesses the islands of Zābaj and al-Rāmnī, as well as many others, too numerous to be mentioned. Furthermore, his rule extends throughout the sixth sea, which is the Sea of Sanf.

70. *The seventh sea: the Sea of China*

The seventh sea, as we have said before, is the Sea of China, also known as the Sea of Sanjī. It is very dangerous, with numerous waves and *khibb*; *khibb* means a violent turmoil in the sea. I use the term which is current in the speech of the sailors of these seas. There are large numbers of shoals among which the ships cannot avoid passing. Every time the sea has a great *khibb* and the breakers increase and multiply, small creatures, four or five spans high, can be seen emerging from it. They are like little Abyssinian children, all of the same size and shape, and they climb on to the boats, but no matter how many there are, they remain completely harmless. When the crew sees them, they know trouble is coming, for their appearance heralds a *khibb*. They prepare to meet it as best they can, some perishing and some surviving.

71. *St Elmo's fire*

Those who escape safe and sound have often seen on the top of the mainmast – called *dūlī* by sailors in the Sea of China and other parts of the Indian Ocean, and *sārī* by mariners in the Mediterranean – an object which has the shape of a luminous bird and spreads a light so brilliant that the observer cannot bear to look at it directly nor distinguish its shape. As soon as the light begins to vanish from the top of the mainmast, the sea becomes calm, the waves and the turmoil of the sea subsiding. Then the luminous object disappears, and it is impossible to know whence it came or how it vanished, but it is a sign of salvation and a proof that safety is nigh. This fact has never been disputed by any of the sailors or merchants who have sailed these waters, whether from Basra, Sirāf, Oman or any others who cross these seas. What we have said about it here is possible, and well within the power of the Creator – May His Power Be Exalted – to rescue His servants from disaster.

72. *Crabs*

In this sea there is a kind of crab more than a cubit in length. They come up out of the water, moving swiftly, but as soon as they touch dry land, all animal functions cease and they turn into the kind of stones that are used to make collyrium and other remedies for the eyes. This is very generally known.

The Sea of China, the seventh sea, is known as Sanjī, and there are many stories of its wonders. We have discussed it in a general way, in those of our earlier works mentioned above that deal with this subject. We also relate the nature of the neighbouring seas.

73. *The Lake of the Ingots of Gold*

The explanation of the expression 'the Lake of the Ingots of Gold' is that the palace of the Maharaja overlooks a little lake, which is linked to the largest of the gulfs of Zābaj. The tide brings seawater into the gulf and the ebb carries away the fresh water. Every morning, the king's treasurer enters with an ingot of gold weighing a certain amount – the exact weight escapes me – and throws it into the lake in the presence of the king. At high tide, the water rises and covers that ingot as well as those which were there before, but the ebb leaves them visible and they shine in the sunlight before the king's eyes, as he sits in his audience chamber, which overlooks this lake.

They continue doing this, however long the king reigns, throwing an ingot of gold into the lake each day. No one touches them, but, at the king's death, his successor fishes out all the ingots, without leaving a single one. They are counted, melted down and distributed to members of the royal household – men, women, children, officers and servants – taking into account the rank and prerogatives of each class. The surplus is distributed to the poor and infirm.

The number of ingots and their weight are written down in a register, where it is said: 'Such and such a king lived so many years and left in the royal lake so many ingots of gold to be distributed among his subjects after his death.' It is a glorious thing in their eyes to have lived a long time and to have left a large number of these ingots.

74. *The folly of the king of Cambodia*

Here is an anecdote of interest for the study of the history and customs of the ancient kings of India. It is the story of a king of Qimār [Cambodia], which is not an island but a kingdom that forms part of India, from which the aloe-wood known as 'Cambodian aloe-wood' is exported. It is composed of a coastal strip and mountains. Few regions of India have a denser population, and its inhabitants are distinguished by the freshness of their breath because, like the Muslims, they use toothpicks. They have a horror of adultery, avoid all indecent behaviour and refrain from alcoholic drinks – although in this last particular they are only conforming to the general practice of the people of India. Their troops are, above all, made up of infantry, because their country has more mountains and valleys than plains and plateaux. The land of Qimār is on the way to the state ruled by the Maharaja, Lord of the Islands of Zābaj, Kalāh [Malaysia], Sarandīb, and so on.

They say that once upon a time a young and thoughtless king ruled over Qimār. One day he was sitting on his throne in a castle a day's march from the sea, which overlooked a great river of sweet water, like the Tigris or the Euphrates. His vizier was standing before him and they were discussing the rich and powerful kingdom of the Maharaja and the large number of islands he possessed.

The king then said, 'I have a secret desire I would love to have satisfied.'

'And what is that, Sire?' enquired his vizier, a wise man who knew his master's impetuousness.

'I would love to see the head of the Maharaja, king of Zābaj, brought before me on a trencher.'

The vizier realized that this idea of the king's had been inspired by jealousy, which had sprung up in his heart, and said, 'O King, I would never have dreamt that Your Majesty could entertain such thoughts. Never have we had any differences with that country, either in the past or in the present, nor has it ever given us any cause for complaint. Furthermore, their islands lie very far from our borders and they have never coveted our country.' Indeed, there is a distance of ten or twenty days' journey by ship between the kingdom of Qimār and that of the Maharaja. 'It would be better for Your Highness', concluded the vizier, 'if no one knew of this project and if Your Highness did not mention it again.'

The king was annoyed and paid no attention to this advice. He disclosed his plans to the generals and principal courtiers. The news spread by word of mouth until it reached the Maharaja, who was a wise ruler, experienced and already ripe in years.

He summoned his vizier, told him what he had heard and added, 'This foolish plan, which rumour has brought us, is the fruit of his arrogance and youth, but the fact that his words have been made public forces us to take action against him, for if he goes unpunished it will affect our dignity and power.'

He ordered his vizier to keep this interview a secret between them and to equip a thousand medium-capacity ships and provide each of them with the necessary arms and troops. A rumour was started that the Maharaja wanted to take a pleasure cruise among the islands, and he wrote letters to the kings of these islands, who were vassals of the Maharaja, announcing that he was going to take a trip for his enjoyment in their domains. At this news, each king made preparations to receive the Maharaja fittingly. His orders having been scrupulously carried out and the preparations completed, the Maharaja embarked and set out with his army for the kingdom of Qimār.

Before the king had time to realize what was happening, the Maharaja had entered the river valley leading to the capital, defeated the army, captured the officers and taken possession of the royal city. Thus the whole kingdom fell into his hands. The Maharaja proclaimed the formal end to hostilities and seated himself on the throne of Qimār. Then he had the former king, who had been taken prisoner, brought before him, together with his vizier.

'Whatever possessed you', he asked the king, 'to think of a plan so much beyond your strength? A plan which even if accomplished would not have made you happier and did not even have feasibility to excuse it?'

The king could give no reply and the Maharaja said, 'If you had added the desire to seize my kingdom and put it to the sword to your wish to see my head before you on a trencher, I would now take reprisals. But you only made one precisely stated threat, which I myself will carry out but at your expense. Then, I shall go back to my own country, without touching anything belonging to your kingdom, great or small. I want to make an example of you to your successors, so that they do not overstep the limits assigned to them by Fortune and so that they learn the value of peace when they have the good luck to possess it.' Then he struck off the king's head.

He then turned to the vizier and said, 'I know you were a good vizier. I am well aware of the advice you gave your master; he should have taken it. Choose whomever you think fit to rule after this ignoramus and place him on the throne.'

The Maharaja immediately went back to his own country without himself or any of his companions laying a hand on anything in the country of Cambodia. When he got back to his kingdom, he sat down on his throne, which looked over the lake known as 'the Lake of the Ingots of Gold' and had the dish holding the head of the conquered king set before him. He summoned all the great men of his kingdom and told them the story of his expedition and the reason he had done what he did. His subjects responded with congratulations and praise.

Then he called for the head and it was washed and scented and put in a jar and returned to the reigning monarch of Qimār, accompanied by the following letter:

'The motive for our expedition was the insolence of your predecessor and the need to teach a lesson to his like. Now that we have reached our goal, we feel that we should send you back this head, for we have no reason to keep it – such a victory adds nothing to our fame.'

When the kings of India and China learned of this, it served to raise the Maharaja in their estimation, and the kings of Cambodia, ever since that time, turn, when they rise in the morning, towards the land of Zābaj and bow to the ground, proclaiming their most profound respect for the greatness of the Maharaja.

75. *A merchant in China*

The ancient kings of China had a regular system of government and let themselves be guided by reason in the fair and just judgements which they gave.

It is said that a merchant from Samarkand in the land of Transoxiana left his country with a rich stock of merchandise and reached Iraq. From there he went on with local goods to Basra, where he embarked for the land of Oman. Then he went by sea to Kalāh, which is about halfway to China. Today, this town is a general meeting place for the Muslim vessels of Sirāf and Oman and the ships from China, but it was different in the past. In those days the Chinese ships sailed to Oman, to Sirāf on the Persian side of the Gulf, and to the coast of Bahrayn, to al-Ubulla and to Basra, while the ships from those countries went directly to China. It is only since it has become impossible to count on the justice of the governors and on the honesty of their procedures that the custom of meeting at this intermediary point has developed.

This merchant, then, sailed with a fleet of Chinese ships from Kalāh to Khānfū [Canton], the port where ships drop anchor, as we said above. The king, having heard of the arrival of the boats laden with merchandise and luxury goods, sent a eunuch who was one of his personal servants and in whom he placed great trust. The Chinese employ eunuchs as collectors of taxes and so on, and there are even people who have their children castrated so that they may attain such positions. The king's eunuch, therefore, went to Khānfū, where he summoned all the merchants, among them the one from Samarkand. They all displayed the merchandise he desired. After having set aside what might be of use to the king, the eunuch made the man from Samarkand an offer that did not satisfy him. The dispute reached such a point that the eunuch gave orders for the man to be imprisoned and harshly treated to force him to accept the price.

The man from Samarkand would not yield, however,

having confidence in the king's justice. He was sent at once to Khumdān [Xian], the royal residence, and stood at the place where plaintiffs gathered. Whoever wished to complain of an injustice, whether he came from a distant country or not, put on a kind of tunic of red silk, and went to the place intended for plaintiffs. From there, one of the high officials of these provinces, entrusted with taking charge of the plaintiffs who after their arrival had gathered at this place, had them sent by the mule-post system about a month's journey away.

This is what happened to the merchant: he stood before the governor of the country in charge of these affairs, who said to him, 'You are embarking on a very serious course, in which you run considerable risk of losing your life. Think carefully whether your charge is well founded. If it is not, we shall consider that you have lied and send you back to the country whence you came.'

This statement was made to anyone lodging a complaint. If the plaintiff lowered his voice, or if it was seen that he became flustered and began to retract what he had said, he was given a hundred blows with a stick and sent back to where he had come from. But if, on the other hand, he proved determined, they took him into the presence of the king, who listened to his statement.

Since the man from Samarkand persisted in his complaint and they saw that he spoke with confidence without stammering or becoming flustered, he was taken before the king, to whom he related what had happened. When the interpreter had explained the matter to the king, this latter gave orders that the man should be taken to special quarters where he was lodged and well looked after.

Then he summoned the vizier and the Minister of the Right and the Minister of the Left. These high-ranking dignitaries, who were perfectly acquainted with both their duties and their powers, exercised their functions during emergencies and in times of war. The king ordered them to write separately to their representatives at Khānfū, for each of them had an agent in every province. They therefore wrote to ask for a report on what had taken place between the merchant and the eunuch. The king for his part wrote in the same way to his viceroy.

Meanwhile, the affair became notorious throughout the country, and the letters brought by the post-mules confirmed the merchant's statement. Along all the roads throughout their territory, the rulers of China have mules with docked tails to carry the post and for official letters. The king immediately summoned the eunuch, stripped him of all the privileges which he had granted him and said:

'You have done an injury to a merchant who comes from a distant country and who, having crossed numerous kingdoms and having passed through the countries of many rulers by land and sea, hoped to reach this country without trouble, trusting in my justice. But you have done to him what you have done, and it is only by the greatest chance that he has not left my kingdom to tell the world of my blameworthiness and lack of honour. If it were not for the length of your service, I would have you put to death. As it is, I shall inflict a punishment on you which, if you understand its implications, is worse than death. I am putting you in charge of the tombs of the ancient kings, because you have proved yourself incapable of governing the living and of performing the duties which I had entrusted to you.'

Then the king treated the merchant well and had him sent back to Canton, saying to him, 'If you are willing to sell us that part of your merchandise which is of use to us, we shall give you a good price for it. If not – you are master of your goods. Remain here as long as you wish, sell as you want and go where you desire.'

And the eunuch was detailed to guard the royal tombs.

76. *An Arab meets the emperor of China*

Among the entertaining stories of the kings of China is that of a man of Quraysh, a descendant of Habbār ibn al-Aswad. At the time the rebellion of the Zanj chieftain was taking place in Basra – something everybody knows about – he emigrated to the city of Sīrāf. He had been one of the notables of Basra and was very rich. He set sail from Sīrāf for the Indian Ocean, and after taking ship after ship and travelling through country after country, he crossed India and finally ended up in China, and went to the city of Khānfū. After that, curiosity led him to visit the royal residence,

which at that time was in the city of Khumdān, one of
the largest and most important cities in the country.

He waited a long time at the gates of the palace,
presenting requests in which he stated that he was of
the family of the Prophet of the Arabs. At last the king
gave orders that he should be allotted a house with
everything he might need and that they should attend
to all his wants. The king then wrote to his viceroy in
Khānfū, telling him to make enquiries and find out
from the other merchants the truth concerning the
man's claim to be related to the Prophet of the Arabs.
When the governor of Khānfū had confirmed the claim
in writing, the king admitted the merchant to his presence and gave him great riches, which he brought back
with him to Iraq.

Now this merchant was an intelligent old man, and
said that when he came into his presence, the king
asked him about the Arabs and how they had managed
to destroy the Persian empire, to which he had replied,
'It was by the help of God, May His Power Be Exalted!
The Persians worshipped fire and bowed down before
the sun and the moon, to the exclusion of God.'

The king continued, 'The Arabs have conquered the
noblest and most extensive of kingdoms, the richest,
the most remarkable for the intelligence of its people,
and the most famous.' Then he asked, 'How do you
rank the rest of the kings of the world?'

'I have no idea,' I replied.

At this, the king addressed himself to his interpreter:
'Tell him that we number five kings. The most powerful of all is he who rules Iraq, for he is located at the

centre of the world and the other powers are grouped about him; also, we call him the King of Kings. After this comes our own, which we consider as the Kingdom of Men, for no kingdom is better governed, none is more reliably administered and nowhere are subjects more obedient than ours. This is why we are the Kings of Men. After us comes the King of Wild Beasts. This is our neighbour, the King of the Turks, for they are among men what wild beasts are in the animal kingdom. He is followed by the King of Elephants, that is the King of India, who is recognized as the King of Wisdom, since all wisdom originates from that land. The last is the King of Rūm [Byzantium], whom we consider as the King of Soldiers, for no country has soldiers with such perfect bodies and such beautiful faces. These are the principal kings. The others are all subordinate to them.'

Then he said to his interpreter, 'Ask him: Would you recognize your master, that is to say the Prophet, if you saw Him?'

'How could I see Him?' I answered, 'since He is with God, May His Power Be Exalted.'

'I didn't mean that,' went on the king, 'I meant his portrait.'

'Certainly,' I said.

The king ordered a basket brought, and it was placed before him and he took out a scroll and said to the interpreter, 'Show him his master.'

I saw on the scroll pictures of the Prophets and moved my lips, silently blessing them.

The king, who didn't realize that I had recognized

them, asked the interpreter to ask me why I was moving my lips.

'I am addressing a prayer to the Prophets,' I said.

'How did you recognize them?'

'By certain events in their lives which are depicted here. This is Noah taking refuge with his family in the Ark when God, who had ordered the waters to cover the face of the whole earth, saved Him and those who were with Him.'

The king began to laugh and said, 'As to the name Noah, you are right, but as to the whole earth being flooded, it is something we know nothing about. The deluge affected only part of the earth and did not reach our country. If what you say is true of your part of the world, the fact remains that we, the inhabitants of China, India, Sind and many other countries and nations as well, are ignorant of it, nor have our ancestors handed us down any tradition like the one you describe. And yet, such an event as the inundation of the earth is sufficiently remarkable to strike fear into the minds of the people, to remain engraved in their memories and to be handed on as part of traditional knowledge.'

I did not dare contradict him and counter his arguments, because I knew he would reject them, so I said, 'Here is Moses with His staff and the Children of Israel.'

'Yes,' said the king, 'despite the smallness of his country and the disobedience of his people.'

'Here is Jesus,' I continued, 'riding on His ass, and the Apostles are accompanying Him.'

'His ministry', said the king, 'lasted very little time – hardly more than thirty months.'

Thus he went on through all the Prophets and Their lives, and said many things of which we have reported only a small part.

This man of the Quraysh, who is known by the name of Ibn Habbār, even claimed to have seen a long caption above each picture, which he assumed gave Their name, country, age, and everything about Their life and prophetic mission.

Then I recognized the portrait of our Prophet Muhammad, (May Prayers and Peace Be Upon Him!), riding a camel and surrounded by his Companions, wearing on their feet Bedouin sandals made of camel hide, and belts made of palm fibre from which hung their toothpicks. I wept. The king, via his interpreter, asked me the reason.

'This is our Prophet and our leader,' I answered, 'our cousin, Muhammad ibn 'Abd Allah!'

'What you say is true,' the king replied. 'He and his people reigned over the noblest of kingdoms, but he did not live to see his empire. That was reserved to those who succeeded him.'

Examining the portraits of the prophets, I saw several, who by joining their first finger and thumb of their right hand in the form of a ring seemed to be indicating, through the position of their hands, that creation is like a circle. Others pointed their index finger to the heavens as if they wished to inspire Creation with the fear of what lies above. The interpreter told me that these were Chinese and Indian prophets.

Then he asked me questions about the caliphs, their appearance and about many of their laws. I answered insofar as I knew the answers. Then he said, 'What do your people believe is the age of the earth?'

'Opinions differ on the subject,' I said. 'Some say 6000 years, others less or more.'

'Is that what your Prophet said?' he went on.

'Yes,' I said.

He burst out laughing and so did his vizier, who was standing there, making it clear that he didn't think much of my answer.

'I don't think your Prophet ever said that,' the king added.

I tried again and said, 'Yes, indeed, it was the Prophet himself.'

I saw the expression of disbelief on his face, and he told the interpreter to speak to me as follows: 'Take care what you say. One does not address kings unless one is absolutely certain of one's facts. You maintain that there is a difference of opinion among you on this subject – you are therefore in disagreement about something your Prophet has said. Now when it comes to what the Prophets have said, differences of opinion are not permissible. On the contrary, everyone must agree without argument. Take great care, therefore, not to mention this matter again, or anything like it.'

He talked to me also of many other matters which time has erased from my memory. Then he asked, 'Why did you leave your king, whose dwelling place and lineage are closer to you than ours are?'

I told him what had happened at Basra and how I

had settled in Sirāf. 'There', I went on, 'I conceived a wish to see you, O king, for I had heard of the prosperity of your kingdom, your wise rule, your justice and the benefits you bestow upon all your subjects. I wanted to reside in this kingdom and see it with my own eyes. Now, God willing, I shall go back to my country, to my cousin's kingdom. There, I shall tell all that I have seen of the majesty of this kingdom, the vast extent of this country, the justice which is extended to all, and I shall speak of your most admirable qualities, O most excellent king! I shall tell nothing but good of it, having nothing to say but praise.'

That pleased the king, and he ordered me to be given rich gifts and magnificent robes of honour, and ordered me to be taken by mule post to Khānfū. He wrote to his governor to treat me well, to assign me a place in the first rank among the distinguished men in his entourage and to give me board and lodging until I should depart. I therefore stayed with him, living in abundance and delight until I left China.

77. *The Skilfulness of the Chinese*

The inhabitants of this kingdom are, of all God's creatures, the most skilful in painting and all the arts. No other nation can compare with them in any craft whatsoever. When a Chinese has completed a piece of work he considers inimitable, he brings it to the king's palace seeking a reward for the beauty of what he has created. The king at once orders the object placed on view in the palace for a year. If during this time no one finds any fault with it, the king grants its maker a recompense and admits him to the company of his artists; but if any blemish is found in the work, the man is sent away without reward.

A certain man had painted on a silk robe an ear of wheat with a sparrow perched on it. The artistry was of such perfection that the beholder really thought it was an ear of wheat upon which a sparrow had alighted. This masterpiece remained on exhibition a long time. One day, a hunchback passing before it found a flaw. He was brought into the king's presence, together with the artist, and he was asked what fault he had observed.

'Everyone knows', he replied, 'that a sparrow cannot settle on an ear of corn without bending it. Here, the painter has shown the ear straight, not bowed at all, although he has perched a bird on it.'

The hunchback was right and the artist got no reward.

Their objective in doing this and similar things is to put the artists on their mettle and force them to take infinite care and pains, and to make them reflect at length on the execution of works they undertake.

78. Rebellion in China

China remained prosperous, thanks to the state of justice she enjoyed, just as she had been under her ancient kings, until the year 264/878. But then an event took place that upset the order of things and overthrew the authority of the law, a situation which has lasted down to the present day, 332/943.

A remarkable man named Huang Ch'ao, who lived in a certain city in China, suddenly rose up in rebellion. He was not a member of the royal family. Evil by nature and seeking to foment unrest, he gathered around him criminals and malefactors. The king and his ministers paid no attention to him at first, because he was unknown and of no importance. But his movement grew in strength and his reputation spread, while at the same time his arrogance and daring increased. Criminals of all kinds travelled great distances to join him, swelling the ranks of his army. Then he went forth and began raiding the villages and towns, until he pitched camp before Khānfū, a major city standing on the banks of a river longer, or as long as, the Tigris. This river [the Hsi River] flows into the China Sea, which is six or seven days journey from Khānfū, and ships from Basra, Sirāf, Oman, the ports of India, the island of Zābaj and Sanf and other kingdoms sail up the river to it with their cargoes and merchandise.

Huang Ch'ao quickly moved to attack Khānfū, in which lived a mixture of Muslims, Christians, Jews and Fire-worshippers, as well as Chinese, laying siege to the city. The king's army counter-attacked, but he put it to flight, capturing the king's womenfolk. His army increased in size, and he took the city of Khānfū by storm, killing a number past counting of its inhabitants. They estimate the number of Muslims, Christians, Jews and Fire-worshippers who died by the sword or were drowned fleeing the massacre at 200,000. We can record this number because the kings of China have registers in which they set down all the subjects of their kingdom as well as those of neighbouring countries that are under their protection. They have agents who are in charge of this census, for they want to be kept informed of the true state of the people over whom they rule.

The enemy cut down the mulberry plantations that surrounded the city of Khānfū and which are maintained with great care, because the leaves of this tree are used to feed the worms that make silk. The destruction of the mulberry trees stopped silk production in China and hence its export to Muslim lands.

Huang Ch'ao went from city to city, conquering them one after another. Whole ethnic groups, some enamoured of the idea of war and pillage, others fearing for their own lives, joined the insurgents. He headed for Khumdān, the king's residence, at the head of 300,000 men, cavalry and infantry. The king marched out to meet him at the head of 100,000 troops, all that remained of his loyal followers. The two armies clashed and fought continuously for almost a month. Both sides held out, then fortune turned against the king and he retreated in defeat. The rebel pursued him, and the king took refuge in a city on the borders of his country.

The rebel gained control of the territory and took possession of the capital. He seized all the wealth and treasure that the kings of old had set aside in case of disaster. Then he devastated the countryside and conquered the cities. Knowing that his low birth disqualified him from rule, he gave himself over to laying waste to the country, looting and pillaging and spilling blood.

On the borders of Tibet, which has already been mentioned, is the city of Mdo. The king shut himself up within its walls and wrote to the Uighur Khan, the ruler of the Turks, to ask for help. He told him what had happened and reminded him of the duties that bind kings to each other, so that when one seeks help from a brother, the other cannot refuse to come to his aid.

The Uighur Khan helped him by sending one of his sons at the head of some 400,000 cavalry and infantry. Meanwhile, Huang Ch'ao's advance became increasingly threatening. The two armies met and the war between them lasted almost a year. A great number from both sides perished, and Huang Ch'ao disappeared; it is said that he either was killed in battle or drowned.

During this war, the governors of the various regions made themselves independent rulers of their provinces, just like the rulers of the various satrapies after Alexander the Great, the son of Philip of Macedon, killed Darius, king of Persia, and indeed, as is happening in our own country today, in the year 332/943.

The king of China had to make do with the nominal obedience accorded him by the governors and the title of king which they granted him in their correspondence. He therefore resigned himself to demanding no more than minimum homage from them, and although they paid him no tribute he allowed them to live in peace. Each of these new rulers attacked his neighbours insofar as his strength and power enabled him to do so. As a result, the order and harmony which had reigned under the kings of old ceased to exist.

79. *Korea*

Beyond the coastal regions of the country of China there are no known kingdoms or countries which have been described, except al-Sīla [Korea] and the islands belonging to it. Only the rare stranger who arrives there from Iraq or any other country ever departs, because the air is so healthy, the water so clear, the land so fertile and goods of all kinds are in such great abundance. The inhabitants live on good terms with the people of China and their kings, with whom they are continually exchanging gifts.

80. *The author addresses his readers*

I finished writing this book in the month of Jumada I of the present year, 336/947, while staying at Fustāt in Egypt. The present holders of power in Baghdad are: Abū al-Hasan Ahmad ibn Buwayh the Daylamite, known by the title Mu'izz al-Dawla; his brother Hasan ibn Buwayh, with the title Rukn al-Dawla, the master of Isfahan and the districts of the Ahwaz and other provinces; and their elder brother, the head of the family, 'Ali ibn Buwayh, with the title of 'Imād al-

Dawla, who is based in Fars. But the one who controls the government of the caliph Mutī' is Mu'izz al-Dawla. It is he who, accompanied by the caliph, is waging war against the Barīdīs in the region of Basra, according to the latest news that has reached us.

In this book, I have in very few words set down numerous happenings and have briefly mentioned events of considerable importance. In any case, each of my works contains information omitted in the book that preceded it, indispensable information of the greatest importance and utility. Thus I have reviewed every century, together with the events and deeds which have marked them, up until the present. Furthermore, there is to be found at the beginning of this book a description of the seas and continents, of lands inhabited and uninhabited, the lives of foreign kings, their histories and those of all the different peoples. If God gives me life, if He extends my days and grants me the favour of continuing in this world, I shall follow this book with another, which will contain information and facts on all kinds of interesting subjects. Without limiting myself to any particular order or method of setting them down, I shall include all sorts of useful information and curious tales, just as they spring to mind. This work will be called *The Reunion of the Assemblies* – a collection of facts and stories mixed together, to provide a sequel to my earlier writings and to complement my other works.

As to the events set down here, they are of the kind that a wise man cannot ignore and which it would be inexcusable to omit or to neglect. If one does no more than enumerate the chapters of this book, without reading each one carefully, the truth of what I am saying will not be appreciated, nor will its erudition be given its due. The knowledge I have gathered together here has cost me long years of painful effort and research and journeys and voyages across the lands of east and west and to a number of countries not under Muslim rule.

May the reader, therefore, be kindly in his perusal of this book and have the goodness to correct such copyist's errors and faults in transcription as may offend him; and bearing in mind the deference and good relations which should exist among scholars and which the intellectual world demands, let him take my situation into account! The author of this book compares himself to a man who, having found pearls of every kind and every shade scattered here and there, gathers them into a necklace and makes them a precious piece of jewellery, an object of great worth which its purchaser will cherish with care.

Lastly, may the reader rest assured that I have not here taken up the defence of any sect, nor have I given preference to this doctrine or that. My aim has been to relate the most notable events in man's history, and I have pursued no other.

THE STORY OF PENGUIN CLASSICS

Before 1946 ...'Classics' are mainly the domain of academics and students, without readable editions for everyone else. This all changes when a little-known classicist, E. V. Rieu, presents Penguin founder Allen Lane with the translation of Homer's *Odyssey* that he has been working on and reading to his wife Nelly in his spare time.

1946 *The Odyssey* becomes the first Penguin Classic published, and promptly sells three million copies. Suddenly, classic books are no longer for the privileged few.

1950s Rieu, now series editor, turns to professional writers for the best modern, readable translations, including Dorothy L. Sayers's *Inferno* and Robert Graves's *The Twelve Caesars*, which revives the salacious original.

1960s The Classics are given the distinctive black jackets that have remained a constant throughout the series's various looks. Rieu retires in 1964, hailing the Penguin Classics list as 'the greatest educative force of the 20th century'.

1970s A new generation of translators arrives to swell the Penguin Classics ranks, and the list grows to encompass more philosophy, religion, science, history and politics.

1980s The Penguin American Library joins the Classics stable, with titles such as *The Last of the Mohicans* safeguarded. Penguin Classics now offers the most comprehensive library of world literature available.

1990s The launch of Penguin Audiobooks brings the classics to a listening audience for the first time, and in 1999 the launch of the Penguin Classics website takes them online to a larger global readership than ever before.

The 21st Century Penguin Classics are rejacketed for the first time in nearly twenty years. This world famous series now consists of more than 1300 titles, making the widest range of the best books ever written available to millions – and constantly redefining the meaning of what makes a 'classic'.

The Odyssey continues ...

The best books ever written

PENGUIN ⊙ CLASSICS

SINCE 1946

Find out more at www.penguinclassics.com